NO FAMILY ALBUM

NO FAMILY ALBUM

CHRONICLES OF A FOSTER CARE SURVIVOR

EDWARD S. BLOTNER

iUniverse, Inc.

New York   Bloomington

No Family Album
Chronicles of a Foster Care Survivor

Copyright © 2010 Edward S. Blotner

iUniverse books may be ordered through booksellers or by contacting:

iUniverse
1663 Liberty Drive
Bloomington, IN 47403
www.iuniverse.com
1-800-Authors (1-800-288-4677)

ISBN: 978-1-4502-1252-6 (sc)
ISBN: 978-1-4502-1254-0 (dj)
ISBN: 978-1-4502-1253-3 (ebk)

Printed in the United States of America

iUniverse rev. date: 02/25/2010

Contents

In Humble Gratitude

I WISH TO EXPRESS THE FULL MEASURE OF MY APPRECIATION TO Ron Huber, a three-time published author himself, for allowing me to tell his gripping tale of rejection, imprisonment, and loss of free will. As my co-author, friend and guide, and fellow early-morning Metro rider, Ron has led me with a sure hand through the wondrous complexities of writing and publishing a book. Without Ron I never would have become an author. Ron's early struggles illustrate the plight of all the neglected children of his generation.

Over my long career in journalism, I have had many different brands of editors—some mean, some green, some lost, some soft. Yet no editor is as committed to my work as the pretty woman I wake up with every morning—my beautiful, outstanding wife, Diana, whose major suggestion here and major suggestion there helped me move the chains closer and closer to the end zone.

My thanks to Barbara Hollingsworth, local opinion editor of the *Washington Examiner*, for allowing me to use material from her explosive columns on abuse at foster care homes.

I want to dedicate this book to our two late mothers, Dora Blotner, who repeatedly urged her deeply shy teenage son to "stand up straight, don't slouch, and look directly into the eyes of the person you are talking to"; and Norma Bagley, whose legacy was a beautiful daughter on the inside and on the outside.

To our combined five children and twelve grandchildren.

To my valuable friend forever, Robin Rupli, who provided her journalist skills and helped me edit my book. My deep appreciation to my colleague and technical and editorial adviser, Hamid Hosseini. Special thanks to Michael Gray and Szabolcs Gyalokay.

To the thousands of former abused foster kids, I hope these chapters will in some small way offer hope that, with hard work and good fortune, even the least fortunate can become positive citizens in one's community.

Last, and decidedly least, to my eighth grade elementary school teacher, Mrs. Hutchinson, who once counseled me in open class against taking the college course in high school that next year. She stood at the front of her desk one day, pointed her two index fingers at me sitting at the back of the room, and decreed, "Edward, you won't make it."

A shocked hush swept across the tiny classroom as my face reddened and my heart pulsated faster. Nobody looked at me. I was saved by the recess bell.

Introduction

IN A SHAMEFUL ORGY OF SOCIETAL EVIL, A TYRANNICAL, DEPRAVED Illinois foster care mother forced a child's head down a brown-stained stinking toilet bowl until he almost shook and gurgled to death.

The same child's second demonic foster care mother reportedly attempted to force his and his brother's hands into a fire that she started in a frying pan, because they were playing with matches. They were also made to "kneel on bricks under the hot sun with bare knees for long periods of time."

In another shadowy foster care home a set of infant foster twins were stashed away in a filthy, darkened room, confined to a dungeon-like cave-crib crudely wrapped with chicken wire and tape. Court records say they often went without food or drink or human contact of any kind.

The brother, Jordan, suffers from brain damage. At birth, shunts were implanted in his brain to drain the fluid. According to a civil rights suit filed in 2007 in U.S. District Court in the state of Oregon, the foster parents failed to provide the toddler with crucial medical treatment, forcing him to smash his head on the side of the crib again and again to ease the pressure.

On the day the police and child welfare workers converged on the foster home to rescue him, little Jordan was almost comatose. At last report, the then six-year-old Jordan had not been toilet trained and could not speak.

The girl, Kaylie, can speak only twenty-five to fifty words. Both suffer from post-traumatic stress disorder and are at the bottom one percent of development for children their age group. The court documents show that due to the severe abuse and neglect, the twins will need close medical attention for the rest of their lives.

The foster parents flatly denied the allegations, claiming that they took the children to all their doctor's appointments and fed them. But the Oregon Department of Welfare Services agreed to set up a two million dollar fund to care for the twins' future, the largest such settlement in the agency's history.

These horrific examples of the frayed components of the human fabric have slashed through generations of our treasured youth in thousands of foster care homes across the United States, where harsh abuses still transpire and where the development of these vulnerable children is curbed, perhaps for a lifetime, amid indications from several experts that our foster care system is in shambles.[1] With an estimated half million children now in foster care homes on any given day across America, and 130,000 waiting to be adopted, a staggering 80 percent of them are "worse off than comparatively mistreated children who remain at home; only

---

1   Statement issued by Representative Jim Mcdermott announcing the signing into law of foster care legislation, October 8, 2008. The bill provides, among other things, federal reimbursement to states choosing to provide assistance to grandparents and other relatives who become legal guardians of children whom they have cared for as foster parents.

children placed in orphanages fare worse and doing nothing" actually does less long-term damage. An 80 percent failure rate should be enough to close down any government program, but social service agencies are rewarded with millions of dollars instead.[2]

Children in foster care homes are more prone to suffering from incidents of behavioral and emotional problems, ranging from expulsion or suspension from school to poor health and even neurological impairment.[3]

Most of these abused, bewildered kids feel the effects of mistreatment long after they are forced from our foster care system at age eighteen.[4] For example, columnist Barbara

---

2 Barbara Hollingsworth's column "The Continuing Foster care Fiasco," March 15, 2009.

3 Report by the Child Data Bank. "Foster Care" no date available. It says, "Children in foster care are more likely than other children to exhibit high levels of behavioral and emotional problems. They are also more likely to be suspended or expelled from school and to exhibit low levels of school engagement and involvement with extracurricular activities. Children in foster care are also more likely to have received mental health services in the past year, to have a limiting physical, learning, or mental health condition, or to be in poor or fair health."

4 Richard Wexler, Director of the National Coalition for Child Protection Reform, reprinted in Barbara Hollingsworth's column in the *Washington Examiner* on March 15, 2009. Barbara says, "Many foster parents are wonderful people who make heroic efforts to ease the suffering of abused and neglected children. But some are like the southwestern Virginia woman described by one of several foster children placed in her care: 'The kitchen and even on the game controllers and floor of the house had the remains of spoiled food and dead insects on the counter tops and floor … we ate meals of ground turkey and rice almost every day. I lost a lot of weight … We weren't the only ones starving, either. The dogs they were emaciated and infested with fleas and ticks so bad that the one dog that was pregnant was so skinny her bones were showing through and we told her to take it to the vet but she said we would make a game out of it and had us pick off ticks … and stomp on them while she laughed …'"

Hollingsworth of the *Washington Examiner* quotes one expert, Richard Wexler, director of the National Coalition For Child Protection Reform, who says that "one recent study of 15,000 foster care alumni found they had twice the rate of post-traumatic stress disorder of Gulf War veterans and only 20 percent could be said to be 'doing well.'"

Mr. Wexler asks, "How can throwing children into a system which churns out the walking wounded four times out of five be 'erring on the side of the child'?" He also says, "On any given day, 30 percent of D.C. foster children are trapped in the worst form of foster care group homes or institutions."

Barbara says,

> Despite evidence that removing children from their homes traumatizes them, millions are still forced to live their lives with strangers or adopted out like shelter pets. One activist recently told Congress that many children are sent to "clearly inadequate" families just so social service agencies can succeed by boosting their numbers. Children like 13-year-old Alexis (Lexie) Agyepong-Glover, who was dumped, still alive, into an icy creek in Prince William County and left to die. Lexie was removed from her adopted mother Alfreeda Gregg-Glover's home despite numerous reports of abuse. She ran away three times in the weeks prior to her death, but the authorities kept bringing her back.

Ask any former foster care child and they will tell you that the pain and the shame never go away. Says one, "It is an incurable disease."

The National Coalition for Child Protection Reform reports that "national data on child abuse fatalities show that a child is nearly twice as likely to die of abuse in foster care as in the general population." As reported by the National Coalition for Child Protection Reform, a "Baltimore study, this one examining case records, found abuse in 28 percent of the foster homes studied—more than one in four." And "a study of cases in Fulton and Dekalb in Georgia found that among children whose case goal was adoption, 34 percent had experienced abuse, neglect, or other harmful conditions. For those children who had recently entered the system, 15 percent had experienced abuse, neglect or other harmful conditions in just one year. Simply put, the Coalition says, foster care is, 'not safe.'"[5]

Yet many foster children manage to navigate the minefields of neglect and frugality and make it through to the other side.

Case in point: Ron Huber, the subject of this book.

Ron Huber was born in 1946, a world shattered by war and riveted by the transition to peacetime. A unified America had led its allies to crushing defeats of a deadly Axis consisting of Hitler's Nazi Germany, Mussilini's Fascist Italy, and Tojo's Imperial Japan.

---

5   The National Coalition for Child Protection Reform also reports that "an Indiana study found three times more physical abuse and twice the rate of sexual abuse in foster homes than in the general population. In group homes there was more than ten times the rate of physical abuse and more than 28 times the rate of sexual abuse as in the general population in part because so many children in the homes abused each other." Report by the National Coalition for Child Protection Reform, "Foster Care vs. Family Preservation: The Track Record on Safety and Well Being," November 11, 2009.

The mighty, victorious Yanks came roaring home on land, from the sea, and in the air from bloodied battlefields in Europe and Asia to deafening cheers at wild, massive ticker-tape parades winding down American flag–draped big city streets. Strangers kissed strangers along Broadway.

The war had pulled us out of the Great Depression and drawn millions of women into the workforce.

As the Red Menace gained traction around the globe, laughter erupted in neighborhood movie houses across America to the shtick of The Three Stooges, Abbot and Costello, and Laurel and Hardy.

We were eyewitnesses to "Da Bums'" new infielder, Jackie Robinson, line driving that "pea" hard to deep left and clear through racial barriers in Major League Baseball, which finally allowed anyone with the skills to play in the bigs. Robinson proceeded to knock the cover off that ball for the next decade. We sat before old-fashioned television sets most every afternoon to see a carved-out stick of wood named "Howdy Doody." We went to public parks to fling the Frisbee around on cool summer nights. We thought we saw scary inhuman figures from Mars lurking around our backyards in so-called UFOs. We saw a mean-looking piece of furniture in our homes that they called a "computer," 1940s style.

Gandhi and Babe Ruth died. The state of Israel was born. A postage stamp cost three cents, a gallon of gas sixteen cents, and a movie ticket sixty cents.

Into the more manageable fifties, America stood by a gallant seamstress who refused to give up her seat to a white man on a bus ride to glory, starting one of the greatest American social revolutions ever. Sputnik, Khrushchev, and the

McCarthy hearings scared the hell out of us. The polio vaccine wiped out the dreaded disease. Elvis shook it all about, and we got caught up in hula hoop craze.

After dinner, families hovered around radio sets in the parlors to listen intently to the breathtakingly whimsical humor of George Burns and Gracie Allen, Jack Benny and Rochester, Bob Hope and Fred Allen, and Phil Harris and Frankie Rembley.

There were plenty of good times for most Americans back then, in this post-war era of national elation.

But not for Ron Huber.

Abandoned by his alcoholic parents, Ron was left frail and traumatized, sent to two foreboding, dungeon-like foster care ghettos. He lived in toxic environments and was raised by two female Victorian despots disguised as foster care mothers over a span of fifteen years. Eventually came the miracle of emancipation and salvation, as our subject emerged in adulthood as a Green Beret, radio personality, multiple published book author, traveling lecturer, high-ranking federal government executive, family man, and most recently, part of Madison's "Who's Who."

Drawing on all his strength and determination, the future Vietnam War veteran struggled up the steep, cluttered path to salvation. But he still carried lifelong emotional scars in his soul and often plunged into an inescapable darkened environment with other un-healable foster care victims, still suffering, still staggering as the unheralded, unnoticed American heroes and legends of our times.

For years, Ron gasped for love and acceptance as "a throwaway child" under a corrupt, broken foster care system that has decimated the lives of untold numbers of kids. Some of them are eventually dispatched to mental institutions, banished to prisons, or forced to sleep each night on a different steamy manhole cover before they feel the cruel whacks from police nightsticks. Other victims walk among us, burdened with deep self-pity and self-doubt, going unnoticed. They pass us by unable to forget. They wince. They cry mournful tears every day, riveted in silent pain and insecurity of a lifetime of heartbreak.

To this day many of them are still trapped in an emotional vise of virtual solitary confinement after surviving in the homes of these hostile, villainous strangers. Their hard-fought triumphs over these humiliating indignities should be celebrated. But instead they go unnoticed, and they live in a dark secrecy for too many years and decades. That must be reversed now. It must come into the open so that society may bear witness.

No national or international figure, Huber takes us on his own life's journey. Cruelly and unceremoniously dumped by their troubled, pathetic, penniless mother and father in post-World War 2 America in a desolate, filthy rat-laden apartment in Rockford, Illinois, Ron, age three, and his brother, Vic, age six, were left with no food, no heat, no electricity, and no place else to go for three long months until a social service worker found them and whisked them off to a children's home. It was in that rundown dwelling where one of his brothers died from a rat bite, while another one was adopted years later. More than a decade later, Ron smashed his way out of this dispirited, darkened life, but he never forgot how he was carted away against his will to these despicable homes, and he is still wrapped tightly in the horrific memories of a broken foster care system.

It was at Ron's second un-nurturing foster home that the child's personality began to take shape in response to his environment. This is described by a Red Cross social worker's report contained in an entry in the official records of the State of Illinois, Rock Island County, dated November 7, 1958.

> Ronald is very needful of relationships and endeavors to establish them. The relationships established are superficial in nature as they are established to satisfy his immediate needs for gratification rather than with the deeper intention of gaining long term genuine friendships. The superficiality is readably observable when Ronald expresses anger and hurt when he does not get his way and translates the obstacle as rejection. Ronald's need-for-love level is considerably below his chronological age. Correspondingly, his absorption and saturation rate threshold is extremely high and seldom ever reached. Hence, he is seen to be always reaching out for gratification. This needful boy is quick to say he is not wanted and has stated so regarding his foster home and school settings. Without doubt there is merit to what he says objectively as well as according to his interpretations. Constant giving above the normal exchange expected may become tiresome or exhausting to school staff and peer groups. A slight cessation of the amount previously extended may be easily interpreted by Ronald as being rejection as well as not being wanted. Ronald does not like his foster mother (Mrs. Borg) and wants to be replaced, "even if

I have go to an orphanage." His main reasons are his foster mother doesn't want him, is always yelling at him, and is too bossy. Other reasons are that he is tired of being isolated on a farm and he can't go anywhere or do anything or make friends easily. Realistically, the farm is in semi-isolation regarding proximity to the nearby community as well as it being true that use of the family car is limited since Mr. Borg drives it to work between 1 and 2:00 PM every day except for weekends. Otherwise Ronald is saying that his total needs have not been met which is true.

In America today, we are witnessing a disgraceful national crisis in foster care, one that is going largely unnoticed. No one seems to care that our society's beleaguered system takes in tens of thousands of orphaned or abandoned children a year throughout the United States, with many of them incapable of adjusting to the regular world, according to a federal government report.

You may ask, "So what? Why should I care about them?" Americans, consider this: How many generations of leaders have we potentially lost from our society's neglect of these unfortunate creatures? How many Jonas Salks have we lost? How many FDRs, Thurgood Marshalls, Sonya Sotomayors, Einsteins, Hemmingways, Chopins, Shearings, Hank Aarons? How many of these unfortunate people are now flooding our prisons and jails as unrepentant repeated murderers, rapists, lifelong drug addicts? How many thugs, gang members, abusive parents, hookers, bar room brawlers, or members of roving street gangs? We as a caring society must take action to eradicate this endless abuse.

This is the reason the Ron Huber story must be told, over and over again, to make the public aware that it must start caring for future generations of children whose lives could be wasted without proper guidance and care.

What you are about to read is the true account of just one of the half million victims of the foster care system today. It is a clear, strong message to other victims of foster care abuse— that they, like Ron, can escape the madness and overcome a lifetime of tears. But they must stay in the hunt and not abandon their goals, or they are lost.

This shocking exposé tells the story of one man's virtual captivity in brutal foster homes as an abandoned, unwanted child, and how he smashed through the steel barriers put up by a hostile world to reach the top of life.

Where's the light? I cannot see.
What will be my destiny?
And yet, will I be loved?

A biting, howling wind was always slapping him in his face. Ghastly demons were always reaching for his throat. The gaping abyss was always the next step he took. And the serpent was always rising before him, stalking him, ready to strike.

His early life in an entrenched madness had been an odyssey for the misbegotten, described in illusionary sketches on torturous landscapes etched in suspension of time and space inside a gallery stuck forever deep into the vast galaxy of his mind.

Where's the light? I cannot see.
What will be my destiny?
And yet, will I be loved?

Vivid recollections of the deprivation and tyranny he faced as a foster child sends unbridled anger reverberating through the pathways of his heart and soul, exploding in a vast mushroom of dark menacing clouds of dispirited longings.

Where's the light? I cannot see.
What will be my destiny?
And yet, will I be loved?

Familiar figures chiseled on ghostly looking corpses creeping out of their graves of those who stole his youth still haunt him decades later. He cannot shake off the shattering torment of his past. The crossroads are still miles away.

Even now he envisions a painting of an unwashed, ill-dressed toddler with tears streaming down his dirt-stained cheeks, sharing a faded putrid linoleum floor in a severe slum, with ravenous rats scooting past his bare feet. Next to him lies the unmoving body of one of his brothers, dead of rat bites.

Where's the light? I cannot see.
What will be my destiny?
And yet, will I too love?

In his desolation he sees a sketch of a young boy wearing rumpled clothes, virtually imprisoned on a farm, lying on his knees in the barn, straining to get to his feet while balancing heavy bundles of hay as "Mama Borg" is wielding a menacing whip.

He sees a gallant soldier trapped, crouching for his life in a fox hole, looking past the fallen bodies in the rice paddies of Vietnam. Where's the VC hiding? He senses their eyes on him.

Where's the light? I cannot see.
What will be my destiny?
And yet, will I be loved?

Chapter One:
The Memory Train

4:42 AM PRETTY CREEPY OUT THERE. NO ONE AROUND YET. THE frigid, still air penetrated his aging bones as his eyes remained transfixed on the black void at the mouth of the tunnel.

Another icy arctic morning.

The powerful swirling winter wind lashed at the sallow face of the solitary figure, slightly stooped and well dressed on the empty platform at the Shady Grove Metro subway station in Gaithersburg, Maryland. He shuddered, shifted his feet, and listened impatiently for the maddening screech from around the bend of the tracks, signifying the arrival of the train that would take him to his federal government job in the capital of Western Civilization. He looked up and read the electric sign: "Red Line, Glenmont, leaving in fifteen minutes."

He glanced feverishly at his watch again as his eyes began to tear and his body started to shiver more violently from the bitter cold. His bundled-up black overcoat and blue scarf that shielded his chunky frame and the red woolen hat that covered his frozen ears and balding head were no match for these savage elements.

On this morning, he suddenly remembered his turbulent youth: how the ferocious winds whipped against the wooden-clapped facade of his second foster home with alarming fury—a run-down, unpainted, severe looking "slave farm" in isolated northern Illinois. It seemed to belong to an earlier age, with dank and crumbling hallways and shadowy rooms, where the temperatures plunged as low as twenty degrees below indoors.

Ron remembered how he and brother, Vic, ran frantically to the outhouse in the middle of night, even in the dead of winter, whenever they had an urgent appointment with nature. Then, in their ill-fitting, permanently stained hand-me-down pajamas, they scrambled like two thoroughbred horses as fast their feet could take them back to the gloomy, tiny bedroom they shared and dove underneath the soiled sheets in constant terror of disturbing "Mama Borg," as they had to call her.

Still breathless, the warmth felt so good. The pillow felt so soft, belying his sense of sheer loneliness for his real mother, wondering where she was getting stinko. But on these nights at least he did not wet his bed, a colossal victory. He also remembered with perfect clarity the scorn "Mama Borg" rained on him and Vic. He thought about the humiliation and physical and emotional abuse they suffered through. He can still feel the outright rejection, the undeserved ear-bending screams, the constant, merciless whippins at her meaty, manly hands and fists. He can never forgive the gross indifference of the dismissive social caseworkers, who were either apathetic or failed to grasp what was happening to them. They did not care to know about Ron and Vic, who dangled on the very edge of our society, prone to falling off at any time. He still shuddered at the memory of one of his foster mothers sticking Vic's head into the filthy toilet bowl because he wet his bed.

He recalled what it was like never to have felt any measure of love as a child. Never a mother's lap, never a mother's love, never a father's tutelage, never a warm, full body hug at bed time. Never a kiss to drive away pain. Never a helping hand, never to be accepted by someone, anyone. Never any of these things to wipe away the deep stains of despair.

His thoughts were interrupted as the rest of the heavily-wrapped, red-faced commuters, made up of mostly federal government workers, began to crowd the platform while its floodlights started to flicker orange, signaling that the subway train was about to snake around the bend of the winding tracks and rumble into the station—*chicka, chicka, chicka, chicka, chicka*—then screech to a stop, open its doors, and let the passengers in.

Ron Huber rapidly stepped into the warmth of the compartment and took the same rear seat near the window that he always took, not talking to anyone especially, not looking at anyone, especially as his pangs of withdrawal were taking over again. But he did notice the small cluster of friendly, talkative men who preferred to stand by the door—made up of Tom Terrific (former football player from Dartmouth), Ray (infantryman of the Gulf war), Noble (the gentle, graceful giant), and Charlie from Damascus.

The conductor's voice blared over the loud speaker.

"Welcome aboard. Stand clear! Stand clear! Doors closing. Red line to Glenmont. First stop, Rockville Station."

Ding, ding.

The subway rolled out of the station and chugged south.

Ron settled in, placed his briefcase by his side along the comfortable brown vinyl seat. He glanced at the front page of one of the local newspapers, which was reporting this morning on the expulsion of two students from a local school for harassing a classmate. He stared out the window into the passing flashes of dizzying white and black images speeding before him in the frigid darkness and rolled back the tears, the fears, and the years of his turbulent childhood.

School, he thought. *My first day of school. How could I ever forget that day?*

Chapter Two:
The First Day of Many

I WAS LIVING IN MY SECOND FOSTER HOME, AND IT WAS MY FIRST day of school. I was so excited I couldn't sleep the night before. Up before dawn, I fed the chickens and the cows. Mr. Borg then drove me to the red schoolhouse along a dirt country road. As I opened the truck door, I glanced back at Mr. Borg, looking for some assurance and encouragement. But Mr. Borg looked away, saying nothing. I frowned and walked into the schoolhouse. Then my excitement turned to horror as the teacher asked me a question that felt like a sharp knife slicing through the flesh of my belly.

I stood there utterly humiliated in the middle of the classroom as the echo of children's laughter rang through my ears. My face felt flush, and my tongue would not work. The teacher, after what seemed like forever, allowed me to sit down. But the damage had already been done. Being branded as "stupid" by my peers for not knowing my own mother's name burned an indelible scar on my soul. They would never know that my ignorance was not the result of faulty memory or mental retardation. I didn't know my mother's name because I never got a chance to ask.

I felt the urine dripping down my pant legs.

Her name was Helen Mae Somerville, but to Vic, Ralph Jr., and me she was a ghost, a shadow, a wanderlust woman who had three marriages and five children that we knew about. The local bar saw more of her than we did. It was very clear that this strange woman did not want us.

A letter written by the caseworker of the Peoria Red Cross dated November 10, 1948, read as follows:

> Mrs. Ralph Somerville had come to the Peoria Red Cross office for advice and help in solving her problems regarding family finances and care for her three children, ages 4 years, 3 years, and 10 months, all boys. Mr. Somerville worked on a boat earning $75 every two weeks. They had been living in a seven room house in Bureau, Illinois, paying $75 a month rent and $30 a month for electricity. The house did not heat properly, and the landlord refused to make the necessary improvements.
>
> The family had many debts, and Mrs. Somerville was embarrassed to go into stores in Bureau. Mr. Somerville was a veteran, and it was thought by the Peoria Red Cross worker that the family would be eligible for planning on the ISSCS, Illinois Soldiers and Sailors Children's Home, program. The mother was said to be quite upset by the whole situation and became emotional during the interview in Peoria. The mother seemed to want to place her children temporarily until

the family could get along financially. No relative could or was willing to help the family.

In a letter written by a caseworker of the Peoria Red Cross, dated November 18, 1948, the caseworker expressed "concern over the family's emergency situation." She included in her report:

> The children were sleeping on the floor in a house that had no heat, and it is necessary that they get out of the house. All of the children are sick with colds, and Mrs. Somerville was so sick the Red Cross sent her to the doctor. The doctor reported afterward that Mrs. Somerville needed rest—that she was not strong enough at this time to work, although the mother said she "has a job in Joliet." As for Ron, the records show his mother describes him as "having no illnesses." The only difference she has noticed about Ronald from the other children is the fact that "he drags one of his legs from running." As yet his mother has never taken him to the doctor to find out what was wrong with it, and she casts Ronald as "a very nervous child."

My grandfather was our primary caretaker. Unfortunately, he was an alcoholic as well and only looked in on us occasionally. On a good day, when he was sober, he would bring us something to eat. If he was feeling especially kind, he would take the extra time to clean our bodies of the horrible stench from sitting in our own excrement for several days. I imagine, though, that it was more for his personal comfort than any sympathy he had for us.

Our pained whimpers were ignored as he raked soap and water over our little bodies, irritating the sores that had developed on our tender backsides. Then he dressed us in clothes that he'd bought from the Salvation Army. They weren't quite as dirty as the ones we'd taken off, so it was a bit of an improvement. After a peanut butter and jelly sandwich and a glass of water, the "nurturing" would be over, and it would often be several days before we saw him or ate again. The rats in the building lived better than we did.

My father, Ralph Wesley Somerville, worked for Federal Barge Lines on a boat named the *Montgomery* over in Chicago. He was often gone for weeks at a time, sending his paychecks home without any thought as to how they were spent. I'm sure he knew that my mother and grandfather were drinking them up. Perhaps he didn't care, but I am more inclined to believe it was because he forgot we were there. He was gone so long that he barely noticed us when he was at home.

Because of our parents' absence, we spent most of our days amusing ourselves on the cold and dirty linoleum kitchen floor. Vic and I, ages four and three, didn't talk much, but rather developed our own method of communication. The two of us did our best to keep our younger brother, Ralph Jr., content. We knew he was just as hungry as we were, but he was usually too weak to cry even if he was upset.

Red Cross entry, dated November 30, 1948:

Mrs. Booth described the mother of the children as an irresponsible person completely uninterested in her children and thoroughly inadequate as a mother. The housekeeping standards were poor and she said the children were as dirty and poorly clothed as one could imagine.

Apparently, there was very little for the children to eat and three of them were like little animals over their food after placements were made.

We lived a dismal existence in those days, but life changed on one blisteringly cold November day in 1948. It was nearly noon, but the sky was dark and menacing. The wind outside was biting and swirled threateningly against the window of our front room, making a loud whirring sound. A battered heater stood in the corner of the room sputtering and creaking but failed to emit any significant warmth. We could see our breath float across the room like puffs of clouds.

From the records of the Peoria Red Cross December 8, 1948:

> Mrs. Somerville stated that she and her husband wanted very badly to be able to provide a good home for their children. But, she added, because of a change in plans in the Bureau they were not able to do this. She feels that putting them on the ISSCS program had been in the children's best interest until she and her husband can get established and get a home for the children. At that time she will want to have them back. Mrs. Somerville was rather emotional about the fact that the Red Cross throughout their contact with her implied neglect of her children and said that was because of this the state would come and take her children away. She emphasized the fact that this was only a temporary arrangement until she and her

husband were ready to move into their new home and one of them could be home.

Mrs. Somerville put no length of time to this proposition. She expressed deep concern on her part and on her husband's part of how their children were getting along at the present time, although she stated that she had not visited or written and did not yet feel equal to this task, although it was explained to her that the children would appreciate her visiting here once in a while. She said she had plans to send fifty dollars to Mrs. Booth for clothing for Christmas presents for her children, although she is very sorry that because she is not paid before Christmas that this will have to be after Christmas.

It was one of those rare days that my mother was at home. Each of us vied for her attention, but she batted us away like flies. When we begged for something to eat, she turned a deaf ear and looked right through us as if we weren't there. Her stare was glassy. It was the look of someone desperately trying to remain sober but close to losing that battle. Sometime around mid-afternoon, a large black sedan slowed to a stop in front of our house. Curious, we perched on the worn sofa and stared out the living room window. We watched as two husky women emerged, struggling against the wind toward our front door. We rushed to tell my mother but found that she was also watching from behind the curtain in the other room. When the ladies reached the walkway, she rushed to the door and let them in. The room seemed to disappear when they stepped inside. Their faces were fixed in a scowl, and they didn't say a word. They looked in our direction and then followed my mother into the kitchen.

I felt a chill that had nothing to do with the cold.

Once inside the kitchen, they spoke in hushed tones. Occasionally someone's voice would rise slightly and cause us to watch the door anxiously. Vic and I were too young to consider eavesdropping and probably would not have comprehended the deal that was being made behind the door anyway. They all returned to the front room a few minutes later. The room remained quiet, and I shifted uncomfortably. I was so nervous that suddenly I felt warm wetness trickling down my leg. Embarrassed, I tried to cover the wet spot. Everyone turned in my direction. My mother stared through me and made no move to clean me up. Both women frowned at me and then shot my mother an irritated glare.

Then, to my surprise, the smaller of the two women marched over to the crib where little Ralph was sleeping. She stared down at him for a moment and then turned and nodded at my mother. Grabbing a blanket that hung across the railing, she wrapped him tightly. She placed a tattered hat on his head, picked him up, and headed toward the front door without saying a word. Vic and I whirled around in my mother's direction expecting her to protest, but she remained mute. Her gaze was fixated on the floor. Confused, I ran to the window and watched as the woman continued to walk down the sidewalk to the car, carrying my brother in her arms.

I'd been so preoccupied with Ralph's fate that I thought not of what was about to happen to Vic and me. A commotion stirred up behind me and regained my attention. I'd completely forgotten about the other woman in the room. To my dismay,

I turned to find her tugging insistently at Vic's arm. He cried and squirmed desperately. I looked from the scene before me to my mother, who still had not moved. It seemed as though her feet were glued to the floorboard. What was going on? I spun back around in my brother's direction in just enough time to see this hulking woman crouch down to eye level and glare menacingly into his face.

"If you don't shut up right this second, I'll smack the daylights out of you!"

The sharpness of her tone stopped Vic in mid-wail. The woman straightened up, yanked his arm, and motioned for me to follow them. My eyes were as wide as saucers, but I didn't say anything. Any ideas I might have had about disobeying faded quickly after hearing her threaten my brother. My eyes welled up with tears, which fell silently down my cheeks. I hung my head and began to walk slowly behind them down the sidewalk to the car.

The huge car door loomed before me. With one final gust of hope, I glanced back toward the front door. My mother stood there gazing through me, cold and indifferent.

Reluctantly, I climbed inside.

A feeling of hopelessness and abandonment swept through me as the car door closed us inside and our front door disappeared from sight. We rode through the city in silence, except for Ralph's occasional squeals from the front seat. Our stomachs grumbled loudly and drew disapproving frowns from the woman, who had finally identified herself as Mrs. Booth. Vic and I tapped each other, pointing and straining to look out of the window. As we continued along the highway, we watched the scenery change from rural fields to bustling city streets.

It was early evening when we pulled up in front of Covenant Children's Home. It was a huge two-story beige brick establishment that stood on the corner of a middle-class neighborhood. The cloud-filled sky cast a gloomy shadow over the building. When Mrs. Booth opened the door and instructed us to get out, I got a sinking feeling in my stomach.

What was this place? More importantly, why were we here?

From the records of the Peoria Red Cross:

The two older Somerville children were placed at the Covenant Children's home on November 19, 1948, and baby Ralph Somerville was placed in the home of Mr. & Mrs. Johnson on the same date.

It had been arranged by Mrs. Booth that the two older children should go to the Covent Children's Home while Baby Ralph could be taken care of temporarily by a family with whom the mother has made arrangements in Bureau, Illinois.

Reluctantly we got out and peered up the stairs at the strange building. Mrs. Johnson stayed inside, holding Ralph Jr. Mrs. Booth walked quickly toward the steps, grumbling over her shoulder for us to come along. She never noticed that we had not moved from our spots on the sidewalk. When she reached the top step, the front door opened and a man emerged. He spoke briefly to Mrs. Booth and then looked down at us.

Reverend Videen was a tall, thin, friendly looking man. He smiled warmly and motioned for us to come closer. It was the first inviting glance we'd seen in quite some time. Vic rushed toward the stairs. I was right behind him, but before I could reach the first step, I let out a faint squeal, and my poor malnourished body collapsed. Vic rushed back to my side, but he was just as frail as I was and could not help. Upon seeing my difficulty, Reverend Videen came down, scooped me in his arms, and carried me inside.

Fig. 2.1.The Children's home

A small hallway and several flights of stairs later, we entered a room filled with several round tables covered with red and white tablecloths. The delicious smell of freshly baked cookies wafted in from the kitchen, and my stomach pitched hungrily.

The reverend took us to a nearby sink and helped us wash our grimy hands before seating us at one of the tables. We sat there expectantly, not saying a word. Minutes later (although they seemed like hours), a smiling heavyset woman dressed in an apron came out of the kitchen and placed two steaming plates in front of us. Both Vic and I sat there, momentarily stunned. Hot food was a luxury that we did not often have. The aroma of the hot turkey and mashed potatoes was intoxicating. I looked anxiously at Reverend Videen.

Were we supposed to eat this? Was it okay?

"Aren't you hungry?" he asked with a puzzled expression. I nodded vigorously, unable to make a sound.

"Please," he urged softly. "Eat up, boys."

No further prompting was necessary. Hovering protectively over our plates, Vic and I immediately began shoveling food into our mouths with our hands. The hot potatoes and gravy burned my tiny fingers, but I barely noticed as I continued to rush scoop after scoop into my mouth. It couldn't have been more than five minutes before the cook returned from the kitchen with a small basket of rolls. Her eyes widened in amazement at our nearly clean plates. She glanced at Reverend Videen, who shook his head sadly. After placing the basket down on the table, she disappeared into the kitchen once more, returning with two cold glasses of milk. By that time we'd eaten everything that had been placed before us. I licked my gravy covered lips and fingers. My stomach groaned loudly for more, but for now that was all we would get.

Mrs. Porter was a petite woman with graying hair and a pleasant smile. Reverend Videen introduced us to her after dinner. Her hand was warm and soft, and my small one felt good inside it. She led us into a bathroom upstairs and deposited us into a warm tub. I couldn't remember the last time I'd been completely immersed in water and had certainly never seen bubbles. Mrs. Porter showed us how to put them in our palms and blow them at one another. We laughed as the white foam landed on our noses and foreheads. Her touch was gentle as she soaped and rinsed us off. The color of the water when we emerged was a dingy gray. Clad in warm pajamas, we padded down the hall behind Mrs. Porter to a large room with many twin beds filled with little boys already sleeping. She pointed to two empty beds and turned back the covers on each one. We slid happily onto the clean, sweet smelling sheets. My face sank into the big, fluffy pillow and I sighed deeply. Vic fell asleep instantly.

Before I drifted off, I remember thinking that if this was only a dream, I didn't ever want to wake up.

Chapter Three:
My First Christmas

In a letter to child welfare in Rockford, Illinois, dated February 9, 1949, Mr. Videen wrote,

Your letter of the 28th was received last week. I believe that plans for the future of the Somerville children should be carefully considered. We believe this because of the condition of the children when we received them and also because of the report on the home from which they came which was given us by the Red Cross through Mrs. Booth. Neither of them had had any training so we had to resort to diapers and rubber pants as soon as they were received. They had to be taught how to eat and how to respect property. When the parents came to visit them, Ronald, the younger child, would have nothing to do with them. He did not remember them, and he seems to be afraid of strangers. I am not sure if he recognized them or just responded to their offer of gifts. After they were gone he asked for them no more. If the children return to their parents and receive the same treatment that they had before, we would consider it very unfortunate for the boys. Victor responded when they offered him some playthings and spent considerable time with them. Everyone here loves Ronald; he is so sweet and Victor has many friends among the children. We hope the children can find a good home.

In a few weeks, I stopped worrying that someone was going to take us away from the home.

Shortly after our arrival, a doctor saw us. I was diagnosed with a severe case of rickets, a result of malnutrition. Having breakfast, lunch, and dinner on a regular basis helped to strengthen my body. I welcomed each trip to the cafeteria, and in those first few days I gorged myself every chance I could.

There were several volunteers that spent their time at Covenant working with the children. Despite their friendly demeanor, Vic and I were initially very withdrawn. But over time, their constant attention and encouragement managed to crack the shell that I'd been enveloped in. Soon I was racing around the playground with all the other children and enjoying it very much.

Lessons became a part of the daily routine as well. Before coming to the children's home, we'd never learned our ABCs. I had difficulty forming words and often became frustrated, opting not to talk at all. Reverend Videen was very concerned about our social and academic development, and he spent a lot of time visiting with us. He was a kind and patient man.

We were shown so much encouragement and love that we began to flourish. The friends that we made with the other children and the staff chased away the pain of hunger and loneliness. Our former life soon became a distant memory.

December brought a beautiful blanket of snow to the city. Snow was something that I usually only watched from our window, since our clothes were never warm enough to allow us to play outside in it. But this year was different! Dressed in thick woolen coats, hats, gloves, and earmuffs, we rolled around with the other kids, making snowmen and snow angels. A snowball fight started after a while. The first time I was hit, it surprised me. The cold ice hit my coat and spattered up onto my face. The blast of air was exciting, and I hurriedly scooped up some snow and packed it into a ball. When I hurled it in the direction of one of the boys we were playing with, it landed perfectly.

Soon after, I became known for my terrific aim, and when teams were chosen I was one of the first ones picked. Having friends was a wonderful feeling, and I looked forward to each opportunity to go outside.

Before we knew it, Christmas was only a few days away. We watched with rapt amazement at the hustling and bustling that was going on. The staff invited us to help with the decorations. The beautiful gold, green, and red garland was silky in my hand and tickled my cheek as I helped wrap it around the branches of the tree. Vic and I had never had a Christmas tree, so decorating it was a new experience. All of us looked into our reflections in the mirrored balls, making funny faces, laughing, and eating more of the popcorn than we were stringing on the tree.

The smell of fresh baked cookies filled the air and tempted our noses while we waited impatiently to get our hands on them. When they were finally ready, we sat down on the floor and sang Christmas carols in between bites of warm cookies and sips of cider.

As it grew closer to Christmas, we watched the other children leave with their parents to spend Christmas Day with them. It seemed strange to us that their parents were taking them home, only to bring them back after Christmas. Nevertheless, the kids bounced around anxiously, waiting to be picked up. Vic and I also waited. I wasn't sure if I wanted to see my mom and dad or not. Perhaps if they came they would want to take us home, too. That was not a thought I relished. However, I did want to see little Ralph. We hadn't seen him since the day we arrived at the home. I often went to sleep wondering if he was having as much fun as we were.

When we came downstairs on Christmas morning, our mouths dropped open. Boxes of all shapes and sizes wrapped in beautiful shiny paper lay all around the tree. The staff had purposely kept the presents hidden to keep us from shaking them, trying to figure out what they were. There was a present for each child who had remained behind.

I stood staring at the beautiful paper for several seconds, not wanting to tear it. I was having a hard time believing it was for me. Finally I slid my finger into a seam and ripped the package open. Vic looked over my shoulder anxiously. He'd already torn into his present and was eager to see what I'd gotten. I lifted the lid of the box. Inside was a knit sweater similar to the one Vic had received. Also inside was a bag of shiny marbles and some candy canes. I smiled and said "thank you," and then we raced outside to play.

Admittedly we were disappointed that our parents hadn't shown up, but since we weren't the only ones that were still alone, the feeling quickly subsided.

In the weeks that followed, the children that had disappeared began to return. Some of them ended up staying with their parents, and our nights were filled with the sniffles of those who couldn't understand why they had to come back. My sniffles came from wondering why we never left.

Chapter Four:
A Surprise Visit

JANUARY WAS BLISTERINGLY COLD. WE'D COME INSIDE AFTER rolling around in freshly fallen snow. My cheeks were red and stinging as the warmth of the auditorium heated them. I pulled off my mittens and wiggled my fingers.

"Hurry up," said Jerry, one of my playmates. We were late for a music class, one of my favorites. There was something about singing that made me forget all about where I was. I hung up my things hurriedly and ran behind Jerry down the hallway. Just as I turned the corner, I stumbled into Mrs. Porter.

"S-s-sorry," I stuttered. I hung my head, waiting for her to chastise me about running indoors.

"I was just coming to get you, Ronnie. Come with me."

My eyes widened with surprise.

Why was she looking for me? Where were we going?

I followed her down the hallway, up the stairs, and into the auditorium. It was empty, and Mrs. Porter's shoes echoed as they clicked across the hardwood floor. There were a group of chairs arranged in a far corner. When we reached them, she instructed me to sit down.

"Am I in trouble?" I asked nervously. Mrs. Porter hadn't said a word since we'd started walking, and I wondered if I'd done something I wasn't supposed to. I wished Vic was there, but he was in a class somewhere. Mrs. Porter stopped rearranging the chairs and chuckled as she looked down at me.

"No, Ronnie. You're not in trouble. There's someone who wants to see you." My heart leapt with anticipation.

Was someone finally going to take us home? Wait! What about Vic?

Just as quickly, my spirits sank. I couldn't imagine going anywhere without my brother. My eyes began to water as I looked around. I wanted to take off running but had nowhere to go.

"Now what are you crying for?"

I almost jumped out of my seat. Reverend Videen had walked up behind me and placed his hand on my shoulder.

"I want to see my brother," I cried.

"What's wrong, Ronnie?" Vic ran into the auditorium at full speed. He slid slightly as he came to a stop in front of me. His face was creased with concern. "Was somebody picking on you?"

Suddenly I felt silly with all three of them looking at me. I wiped away the tears with the back of my hand and sniffled loudly.

"No, I'm fine," I answered quietly. Mrs. Porter handed me a tissue and I blew my nose. The sound of clicking made me look up again. A man and a woman were hurrying across the hardwood floor. It was my mother and father.

"Mother!" Vic bolted from the chair next to me and ran in their direction. My mother rushed to meet him. He crashed into her arms, and she hugged him tightly. I watched with a puzzled expression. I couldn't remember my mother ever being that affectionate. Had something changed?

My father walked over and stood awkwardly in front of me holding two bulky packages. I looked up at him. His face was unshaven and worn looking. His eyes were expressionless, and they made me shiver slightly. He was looking at me as if he didn't know who I was. I wanted to crawl under the seat, but by that time my mother had come over. She was still hugging Vic when she reached down to me.

I cringed slightly from her touch. I wasn't sure if I wanted her to hug me or not. Part of me wanted them both to go away and never come back, but the other part of me wanted to race upstairs, pack my few belongings, and go home. My need for affection won the battle, and I stood under the warmth of her embrace, hoping that maybe something was different. Maybe we really were going home.

"Just look at the two of you!" My mother took a step back and gave Vic and I the once-over. She was beaming as if we'd only been away at summer camp.

"Got something for you," she cooed, reaching and taking the packages from my father. She thrust the two odd-shaped packages at us and continued to smile nervously.

Vic grabbed his package anxiously and began tearing off the paper. I hesitated and looked up at my mother carefully. She looked thinner than I remembered. Her face seemed to have more lines in it. Though the smile was still fixated on her face, she seemed to lose interest in us after handing us the presents. Her foot tapped impatiently as she watched Vic open his gift.

I wanted to hug her again to see if she really was glad to see us, but she didn't look my way again, and she kept her arms folded. My attention was diverted by Vic's squeal. He'd gotten a shiny red fire truck. He plopped down on the floor and rolled it around, making siren noises.

"Open yours, Ronnie! Hurry up!"

I traced around the face of the Santa Claus on my wrapping paper and looked around. I didn't really want to open the present. What I wanted was for mother and father to sit down. I wanted someone to tell me that we were going home now. Even though things at the home had been going well, I wanted Mother and Father to tuck me in at night. But instead they stood in front of us. My mother's initial display of affection seemed to have swept out in the same gust that she'd rushed in with.

"Open your gift, Ronnie." My father's voice broke the silence. They were the first words he'd said since he arrived. I was embarrassed. Everybody was watching me. I tore into the paper with mild enthusiasm. I'd also received a truck. I sat it in the floor in front of me and looked around. My mother and father were engrossed in a conversation with Reverend Videen. They had already put their gloves back on.

"We couldn't come on Christmas," my father explained.

"No money for presents, ya know," my mother added.

Reverend Videen nodded absently. He was looking over at us. Vic had barely looked up from his truck, but I was watching the grown-up conversation intently.

"Perhaps you'd like to join the boys for lunch," the reverend suggested. "I'm sure the boys would love to show you some of the projects they've been working on. You'll be pleased with the progress they've made." He'd barely been able to finish his sentence before my father began shaking his head.

"We can't stay."

Any hope I had about leaving that day was extinguished. Even Vic stopped what he was doing and stared. Reverend Videen stopped trying to persuade them. My mother came over, patted us on the head, and murmured for us to "be good." My father looked at us distantly, and then they were gone.

My feelings crushed, I stood up and walked over to the big window and looked outside. I watched as they hurried down the walkway, got into an old, beat-up looking car, and drove away. I would not see my mother again for decades—just once again, briefly, before she died.

Mrs. Porter had silently returned. She reached for my hand and pulled me away from the window. The tears streamed down my face as she hugged both Vic and me. She held us for a long time before taking us over to the cafeteria for lunch. Neither Vic nor I ate very much during lunch or dinner. I couldn't stop thinking about the other children that had gone home with their parents during Christmas. What was so different about Vic and me that made our parents not want to take us with them?

What was so bad about us that nobody had come for us yet?

I cried myself to sleep thinking that we'd never leave the home, and for the first time in a long time, I wanted to be anywhere but there.

Red Cross entry, dated November 30, 1948:

Mrs. Booth gave some information about the Somerville family in a most critical and condemning way. She did not seem to have an interest in or sincere sympathy for the mother of these children and showed little understanding of a child's particular needs. Mrs. Booth described the mother of the children as an irresponsible person, completely uninterested in her children and thoroughly inadequate as a mother. The house keeping standards were as poor. She said the children were as dirty and poorly clothed as one could imagine. Apparently, there was very little food for the children to eat and all three were like little animals over their food after the placements were made. Objectively, Victor and Ronnie, not having been toilet trained at the time of placement when they were 3½ and 2½ years old respectively, is suggestive of problems existing. The parents' attitude regarding problems the children may have presented is not known. But the inferred impression is that they were not able to handle them through a lack of insight and understanding. An example: Mrs. Booth cited efforts to cope with the children on the toilet for hours. The effort was unrewarding.

Chapter Five:
The Siedemans

IT WAS ESPECIALLY DIFFICULT TO BOUNCE BACK AFTER THE disappointment of my parent's visit. Initially I became quite despondent, falling back in my lessons and not wanting to play with the other kids. But as time passed, I slowly returned to my usual self. Along with the success in our lessons, Vic and I were becoming pretty self-sufficient. We had never received positive feedback from anyone before we arrived at the Covenant Children's Home. For the first time we had a reason to feel proud of ourselves. We had learned to keep our area clean, along with the other twelve boys in our room. We also learned to fold and put away the clothes we received from donations to Covenant. We were so impressed with our new jeans, tee shirts, and shoes that we wanted to keep them looking nice.

Our communication with others had gotten much better. Although at times we were still very shy, our confidence grew a little more each time we received an approving nod or smile from one of the staff members.

Vic and I were now three- and four-years-old, and our lives had become so much better. I wished it would never change, but unbeknownst to us our lives were about to take another major turn.

One cool spring day, Reverend Videen woke us a little earlier than usual. We dressed quickly, anticipating the outing that we were about to go on. He'd said that we were going on a "vacation." The other kids were still sleeping, so we felt privileged to be going somewhere all by ourselves. I watched as he quickly took our clothes from the drawer and placed them into a large, black nylon bag. When I realized that he was taking all my clothes, I stopped dressing and sat down on the bed.

"Let's go, Ronnie," Reverend Videen whispered.

I shook my head. Vic stopped tying his shoes and looked at me. When I pointed toward the bag that held our clothing, he dropped his laces and shrugged.

"What's the matter?" Vic asked.

"He's taking them all," I whispered. "All of our clothes are in there."

A familiar sensation of dread rushed through me, and I ran to hide in the bathroom. I knew there was more to the story than Reverend Videen led us to believe, and as I usually did when I became nervous, I wet myself. When I returned, Reverend Videen was waiting, but my brother was gone. So was the black bag.

"He's in the car already," said Reverend Videen. "C'mon, everything's going to be fine."

He smiled warmly and held out his hand. I took it reluctantly, and after looking around the room one last time, I followed him out to the car.

The sky was gray when we stepped outside. The sun was beginning to peek out and the air was cool. A car waited at the end of the walkway.

When Mrs. Booth stepped out, I began to cry. Reverend Videen wasn't going with us, and that scared me. Vic had already gotten into the car, but when he saw how upset I was, he jumped out and started to cry too. The reverend hugged us both tightly and told us to be good. He wiped our faces with his handkerchief and helped us into the car. I watched sadly from the window as we drove away. He waved to us. I waved too, until he disappeared from sight.

Mrs. Booth was a little different on this ride. She talked to us about the things that we'd done at the home. We warmed up to her as we described the friends we'd made and the things we'd learned. She listened and laughed at some of the funny stories we told. My uneasiness settled down.

We rode for quite some time. Just as my eyes started to droop, we stopped and had breakfast. She treated us to pancakes and bacon at a diner near the road. I piled syrup on my pancakes until there was a small lake on my plate. It tasted so good!

When we got back on the road, I fell asleep immediately and didn't wake up until I heard a car door close. I sat up and rubbed my eyes. I nudged Vic.

A small cottagelike house stood in front of us. Mrs. Booth came around to the back door and motioned for us to get out. She grabbed our bag and lugged it to the front door, where a thin woman in a blue dress with tiny yellow flowers answered the bell. There was a white apron tied around her waist, and her hair was tied up in a messy bun. She smiled at us and held the door open.

Her name was Mrs. Siedeman. She led us into a small living room furnished with shabby brown furniture. We sat down on the sofa and looked around nervously. After instructing us to behave ourselves, Mrs. Booth went into the kitchen and spoke privately to Mrs. Siedeman. As soon as they left the room, Vic and I wandered around the room. There was a bookcase in one corner and a scratched wooden table with dingy lace doilies on it.

A dusty phonograph player caught our attention and we both rushed over to it. Our curious fingers touched the smooth, black vinyl record that rested on it. We were both so engrossed in trying to figure out how this new thing worked that we didn't hear Mrs. Siedeman come up behind us.

"Don't touch that!"

We jumped, startled. Our faces became long and nervous. I cringed slightly, waiting for her to unleash an angry tirade on us, but she didn't. Instead she wagged a warning finger at us and told us not to touch anything without asking first. Then she turned on the phonograph while we watched with interest. She placed the needle on the spinning record, and when music began to flow through the speakers, Vic and I looked at each other with surprise. This thing was very different from the radio that we'd seen at the home. Mr. Siedeman came home while we were listening to music. He was a smallish man, with thick glasses and a bushy mustache. He reached out his hand to us. I stared at him, wondering what he wanted.

"When you meet someone," he said patiently, "you shake his or her hand, like this."

He took Vic's hand, placed it in his own, and gave it an exaggerated shake. He turned to me next. I placed my hand in his and copied what I'd seen Vic do.

Fig. 6.1 Vic and Ron at the Borg farm.

"My name is Otto. You've already met my wife, Mary. You can call us Papa Otto and Mama Mary, or you may call us Mother and Father. You may not call us by our first names only. Do you understand?" We nodded vigorously.

They showed us around the house, ending in a small room toward the back. There were two twin beds, one on each side of the room. They were covered with racing car bedspreads. We ran eagerly to them and jumped on top. Mrs. Siedeman watched us for a moment and then showed us a tall, dark dresser that stood in the corner.

"This is where you will put your clothes." She left us to explore our new room. It felt strange for Vic and me to be the only ones in the room. After having shared our space with so many other kids, it almost seemed lonely. I stepped inside of the closet and squatted in the corner. Tears welled up in my eyes. Though I'd wanted us to have a place of our own, I wanted to go back to the home.

Chapter Six:
Bad Boys

WE'D BEEN LIVING WITH THE SIEDEMANS FOR A FEW WEEKS AND were getting accustomed to their routine. Our mornings consisted of eating breakfast with Mama Mary and then helping her around the house. She was meticulous when it came to cleaning, and I often had to do things over.

One day we were oiling the wooden tables when Vic took the oil over to the phonograph. He began to wipe the wooden case. He poured more oil onto the rag, and some of it spilled onto the record inside. Vic became nervous and tried to wipe it up quickly, but when he saw how shiny the record became from the oil, he poured on more oil and wiped it. I came over and watched. The record looked really clean to me, so I picked up the others that were stacked neatly on the floor. I poured on oil, just as I'd seen my brother do, and began to wipe also. Pretty soon, we'd done every record in the stack, and were feeling pretty proud of ourselves.

Mama Mary came in while we were sitting in the floor admiring our work.

"What have you done?" she scolded, picking up one slick vinyl record after another. My smile faded. Her voice had taken on that shrill pitch that had become too familiar. She was angry with us again. I knew it was only a matter of time before she called Mrs. Booth to come and take us away.

"Go to your room," she ordered.

We slunk away to the solitude of our bedroom. Neither of us spoke. We could hear her hurrying around the room muttering to herself. I curled up inside the closet. It had only been a week since I'd stopped sleeping there to feel safe. Now with Mama Mary being upset with us, I didn't want to be seen. Vic cried openly as he lay across his bed. I listened from inside the closet and cried too.

Sometime after noon, Mama awakened us for lunch. Vic and I were eager to get something in our stomachs and hoped that her anger with us had subsided. After washing our hands, we clamored to the table expectantly. In the middle of the table were a few crackers and some cheese on a plate. The plastic cups we normally used were halfway filled with water, instead of milk or juice. Mama was in her bedroom. We looked around the empty kitchen. There were no other plates lying on the counter. After a few moments of waiting, we realized that this was to be our lunch.

It only took minutes to devour the scant plate of snacks. The water in our cups wasn't nearly enough to wash away the dryness from the saltines and thick cheese, but Mama never came into the kitchen. I guess we weren't supposed to ask for more.

Carefully we placed our dishes in the sink. I looked at Vic, then toward the door, which led to the hallway. When he headed in that direction, I followed. Mama had not released us from our punishment. Sadly we trudged back to our room. I retreated to the closet and played with the small green army men that we'd been given a few weeks ago.

After a while Vic came and joined me. Hours passed, and daylight disappeared from our room. Mama had not so much as looked in on us, although we'd caught glimpses of her as she passed our door several times. Eventually we fell asleep again. There was nothing else to do.

It was well into the evening when I felt Papa Otto's strong arms carrying me from the closet, where we were hiding. He placed me inside my bed and covered me up. He leaned over and tousled my hair affectionately. I pretended to still be asleep until I heard him leave the room, then opened my eyes and looked into the shadows. I heard Vic's even breathing as he slept in the other bed. I climbed out of bed and stood beside him, hoping he would wake up.

I was hungry. Neither of our parents had bothered to wake us for dinner. When Vic didn't wake up, I shook him. He whined and turned over, ignoring me. I looked back at my bed. My stomach growled loudly. I couldn't wait until morning.

Silently, I crept to the kitchen. The refrigerator loomed large before me. I had never been able to open it by myself before—it was too high. I jumped and reached for the handle. I hung on and pulled hard. It didn't open, so I tried again. This time the door swung open so hard that it hit the cabinet and I fell down. I looked inside for something to eat. There was a plate of fried chicken wrapped with plastic wrap on the top shelf. My stomach grumbled with anticipation. I stepped on the bottom of the refrigerator and grabbed the plate. Suddenly my foot slipped. I fell backward into a chair, knocking it over. The plate flew out of my hands and hit the floor with a loud crash, breaking into several pieces.

Lights came on in the hallway, and Papa and Mama came rushing into the kitchen. When they turned on the light and saw the mess on the floor, they frowned.

"What are you doing in here?" asked Mama, her voice sharp. I began to cry. She came over, reached down, and stood me up.

"Look at this mess!" she sputtered.

"I was hungry," I stammered through my tears.

"We do not sneak around in this house, mister! You missed dinner because you and your brother did not know how to behave. Now, clean this mess up right now! I don't work all day cleaning this house for you to mess it up whenever you want."

She crossed her arms and stood glaring at me. I looked pleadingly in Papa's direction, hoping he would convince her to be sympathetic, but he said nothing. He looked at me blankly before turning and heading back to his bedroom.

I squatted down and began to pick up the scattered food. When I looked up again, Vic had padded into the kitchen and was reaching behind the refrigerator to get the broom from the corner. He swept up the broken dish. As I held the dustpan, my stomach groaned loudly. Vic stopped and looked at me for a moment and then continued sweeping, ignoring the sounds of my hunger pangs.

We finished a few minutes later, and Mama came to make sure that the kitchen was immaculate again. Each of the chairs at the table was pushed in, and the place settings were spaced evenly. The towels were folded neatly on the counter. Everything was in its place, and the floor was swept clean. When she was satisfied that there was nothing left to do, Mama turned off the light and led us back to our beds. I crawled under my covers and lay there, sad, alone, and hungry.

When the morning came, I ate everything I could get my hands on. I'd been messing up so much that I worried that things were about to go back to the way they were before. Part of me expected the black sedan to pull into the driveway at any moment to take us back to Covenant Home.

Vic looked at me curiously as I gulped down my milk. Silently he handed me a piece of his bacon, and I munched it down quickly.

"Stop eating like a little pig, Ronald!" Again, Mama's stern gaze was directed at me. It stopped me mid-chew. Victor looked from me to her and frowned. Without a word, he jumped up from the table without clearing his mess and ran out the back door.

"Get back in here," yelled Mama. My eyes were wide with amazement. I waited for Vic to come back, but he didn't. I didn't know what to think. He had never acted like that before. It wasn't like him to defy an adult. I put my dishes in the sink and wiped my place before running out the door behind him. I found him sitting outside under a tree, pulling at the grass. He had a scowl on his face.

"What's the matter?" I asked, plopping down next to him.

"Don't like it here. She's mean to you," he answered without looking up. "I want to go home."

"You mean back to the home?"

"Nope, I mean back to our home. Back with Mommy and Daddy."

I didn't say anything. I had long since stopped thinking about going back to our parents, and it surprised me to hear that Vic still thought of it. Our situation with our parents was far worse than it had been at Covenant or even with the Siedemans.

"Why?" I asked quietly.

"She's mean," he hissed. "I don't like her."

I nodded silently. He was right. She was mean and I didn't like her either.

Mama was furious with us when we finally came in the house. She threatened to send us to bed again without supper. This time Papa stopped her, but by the time we sat down at the table, my appetite had disappeared. I excused myself, went to my room, got down on the closet floor, and went to sleep. Sometime later, Vic curled up beside me, and we slept there until morning.

Chapter Seven:
Going Downhill

WE SPENT MORE AND MORE TIME IN OUR ROOM, PUNISHED FOR doing things wrong. We were never sure if we did anything right.

According to the social worker's report, Vic and I would draw with our crayons on the walls and tear our sheets. The report also mentioned that Vic didn't want to go to kindergarten; what it didn't mention was that he didn't want to go because a bully was giving him trouble at school. Again no one would listen to what we had to say.

Mama yelled almost every day, and it made us both nervous. As a result, Vic occasionally began to wet himself, which only made Mama yell more.

One day the yelling stopped. We'd been invited to dinner as a family over at the house of some friends of the Siedemans. It was one of those very rare occasions where we were able to get out of the house on a social outing. As we got closer to Mr. and Mrs. Fried's house, Mama repeated the instructions that she'd given us earlier.

"You … will … not … touch … anything! You will not speak unless spoken to! You … will … keep … quiet! And, you will eat … everything … on your plate. Do you understand?"

We nodded, but since she was in the front seat, she didn't see us. She whirled around, leaned into the backseat, and got in our faces.

"Did you hear me?"

Our heads bobbled vigorously up and down. It seemed that each of our tiny voices was lost somewhere deep in our throat. Luckily for us, we'd arrived in the driveway. Mama turned back to the front and composed herself, and by the time Mrs. Fried came out to greet us, Mama had transformed into a soft-spoken, smiling woman that we had never met.

"Well, aren't you two handsome little boys?" Mrs. Fried bent over in front of us and smiled.

She was an older woman. Her eyes wrinkled up when she laughed, and her hair was almost silver. Though she seemed nice, neither of us said a word. We simply stood there looking at her through bug eyes until Mama pinched both of us.

"Say thank you," Mama said through clenched teeth. We both mumbled a "thank you." Mrs. Fried laughed and then led us all into the house.

As soon as we entered, the aroma of something delicious tempted our noses. Our house had never smelled this good. My stomach growled loudly, for which I received another pinch from Mama.

"At least I know somebody's hungry!"

Mama laughed politely at Mrs. Fried's joke, but her expression told me that she wasn't pleased. When we walked into the living room, Mr. Fried was sitting in a big brown chair watching television. He jumped up when he saw us and shook Papa's hand. Mr. Fried was a very short and round man. He was bald, with a graying beard. He wore suspenders and a pair of gray trousers. He sort of reminded me of the pictures we'd seen of Santa Claus.

"Please, have a seat," he said, pointing to a blue sofa covered with plastic.

Mama and Papa sat down, but when Vic and I tried to climb onto the sofa as well, Mama frowned at us sternly.

"You two sit down there!" She pointed to a space on the floor at the corner of the sofa.

Without a word we did what we were told. We watched the television while the adults talked.

The smells from the kitchen were dizzying. We hadn't eaten since breakfast, which I couldn't understand. We hadn't done anything wrong that day, yet Mama still hadn't fixed us any lunch. Again my stomach groaned loudly. I stole a sideways glance in the direction of the grownups, expecting to see Mama glaring at me, but luckily she hadn't heard me that time.

After what seemed like forever, dinner was finally ready. It was all we could do to keep from bolting to the bathroom to wash our hands, but we knew behavior like that would elicit a sharp scolding. Somehow we managed to make our way calmly to the table, and when we did, my eyes widened with surprise. The table was covered with food, and it wasn't even a holiday. Lucky for us, Mrs. Fried served us our plates, and she'd heaped them both with food. I'd been worried that Mama would only give us a little and we'd be unable to ask for more.

There was pot roast and chicken! Potatoes, dressing and gravy, corn and other vegetables, homemade rolls! For dessert there was chocolate cake. Everything was wonderful. I wasn't sure about Vic, but I was ready to stay there forever.

Dinner went well, and we were quite proud of the fact that we hadn't received one reprimand. But then it happened.

Vic finished eating before I did. Before he got up from the table, he made sure to excuse himself. Then he pushed his chair from the table and carefully reached for his plate. But his shoes were untied. After two steps, Vic tripped and went sprawling to the floor, the plate crashing down with him.

I gasped, thinking of the plate I'd broken weeks ago. Vic jumped up quickly, breathing heavily, his eyes wide with fear. So were mine. Mama got up quickly from the table and stood in front of him.

"It's okay," said Mrs. Fried from behind them. "It was only an accident."

Mama's eyes narrowed as she stared down at Vic, her back still toward our hosts. I held my breath, wondering what she would do. The wait was unnerving. Vic wet himself, standing right there in front of her. My mouth dropped open. It had been a while since he'd last done that. I was sure that Vic was going to get it, even in front of company.

But Mama surprised us both. Instead of yelling, she turned and gave a weak smile and politely asked Mrs. Fried for a broom. Next she cleaned up the broken dish. Vic and I tried to help, but she brushed us off.

"Nonsense, boys. It was only an accident."

To say that we were shocked would be an understatement. Neither of us knew what to do. I looked over at Papa, but he didn't say a word. Mama cleaned the entire mess by herself. We gathered our coats once Mama finished helping Mrs. Fried with the kitchen. She apologized for not being able to stay and visit, but since she didn't have an extra set of clothes, she didn't want to be rude and have Vic there as he was. Both of us were sure that we were in for something once we got in the car.

Again, nothing happened.

We climbed in and waited anxiously, but Mama still didn't say a word. Before long, the sleep monster fell upon us, and since it seemed we had nothing to worry about, we slept soundly all the way home. Papa carried us into the house and placed us into bed. I yawned sleepily and turned over after he pulled my shoes off and covered me up. I heard him creak down the hallway and then the soft click of the bedroom door closing. I smiled. It had been a good day.

Just as I was drifting off again I heard the door swing back open, and Mama's swift steps filled the quiet. I didn't have to turn around to know that she was coming to our room. There was something about the way she moved that meant trouble.

"Get up!" she yelled, as she flipped on the light in our room. My body tensed as I turned around to see her scowling expression. But it wasn't directed at me. She descended on my brother like a hawk and yanked back the covers. Vic awoke with a start, his eyes wide with fear.

"I said, get up!" She snatched his arm and dragged him to the floor. I watched with amazement as she continued to pull him by the arm down the hallway. I could hear Vic's screams and Mama's screams, and it kept me frozen in one place. I waited for the inevitable sound of yet another smack to his bottom, but when it didn't come, I inched to the doorway and peered down the hall.

"This is where you use the bathroom!" Mama screamed, pointing to the toilet. "You ... do ... not ... embarrass me in front of other people, by exercising absolutely no discipline! People will think I haven't taught you a thing!"

I'd never seen her quite as angry as she was at that moment. She had Vic by the collar of his pajamas and was shaking him violently. Vic was in such shock that he'd fallen silent. This infuriated her.

"Do you hear me talking to you?"

Then to my shock, I watched as she dunked my brother's head into the toilet. The water splashed. His body wiggled and his arms flailed as he searched for something to hold on to. She lifted him up to more of her screams.

"I asked you a question, boy!"

Coughing and sputtering, Vic couldn't get a word out if he tried. This was unacceptable to Mama. Again she submerged him, and it was then that my own scream came to life.

"Stop it! Papa, help!" I ran to their bedroom and pounded furiously on the door. Where was he?

After what seemed like forever, Papa emerged, sleepily rubbing his eyes. His hair was disheveled. How could he have been sleeping through this?

"Ronnie! What in the world?"

"Y-y-yes, M-m-mama!" Vic's stuttered response stopped Papa short, and he strode quickly past me to the bathroom. I followed close behind. The sight of my brother made me gasp. His hair was sopping wet, and he was crying hysterically and coughing all at once. Mama still had him by the collar.

"Mary!"

Mama whirled around in Papa's direction. Her mean glare made me shrink further behind him.

"Let the boy go!" His voice was firm and commanding. I stared up at him. I'd never heard him raise his voice at her.

Mama reluctantly let go of Vic's collar, and he slumped to the floor. She gave him one last glaring look and pushed past Papa and me to her bedroom. The door slammed forcefully. He rushed over to Vic.

"C'mon, Vic, get up."

He lifted Vic in his arms and carried him to our bedroom.

"Ronnie, go get me a towel."

I raced to the linen closet, grabbed a large towel, and raced back. Vic's teeth were chattering, and his eyes were still wide with fear. Papa wiped his head dry, as he peeled the pajama top off of him.

"Ronnie, get Vic some dry pajamas."

I hurried over to the dresser that we shared and got out some dry pajamas. I watched as Papa dressed him. His teeth were still chattering as he tucked him under the covers, and I was still stuck in my spot, watching it all.

"Okay, Ronnie, get into bed now. Both of you get some sleep."

Reluctantly I crawled back into my bed and pulled up the covers. When I was settled, Papa turned out the light and walked out. I listened as the bedroom door opened and softly closed.

Was that it? Didn't Papa care?

He hadn't hugged us or reassured us that everything would be okay. And now we were supposed to go to sleep? I didn't understand. I could tell from the sniffles coming from Vic's side of the room that he was just as terrified as I was of what came next.

"Wanna sleep with me?" I whispered into the darkness.

"Unh unh," he whispered back. His voice was husky, still clogged with water.

We fell back into silence and didn't speak anymore, but I'm sure neither of us fell asleep.

Fearfully we stepped into the kitchen the next morning but found it empty. Our breakfast was on the table, and it was a feast. There were pancakes, eggs, and bacon, with orange juice to drink. Papa's truck was gone, and the door to the bedroom was closed. We figured Mama was locked inside.

We sat down to eat hurriedly, taking nervous glances over our shoulder, expecting Mama to descend upon us at any moment. But she never arrived. We cleared our places and cleaned up as best we could. After doing our chores, Mama still had not come out of her room, so we went outside.

Vic was extremely quiet. He sat on a rock in the middle of the dusty driveway and stared into the ground. He didn't want to play any games, and while I understood, it was boring with him being so solemn.

Lunchtime came and we still had not seen Mama. Again our food was waiting on the table and in abundance. We ate quickly and disappeared into our room until Papa came home. We heard Mama finally come out, but she walked directly past our room and didn't even look in. My heart quickened, then slowed back to its normal pace. The smells of dinner rumbled my stomach, but we were both hesitant about coming out of our room. Papa finally called us to the table, and we trudged slowly into the kitchen. When we reached our places, he said the blessing and we began to eat. Vic and I looked at each other curiously over Mama's absence from the table, again. We all ate in silence.

For almost a week, Mama stayed out of sight. We began to relax, although getting to sleep at night was still difficult. When we did finally see her again, nothing was said about the bathroom incident. Mama even seemed to be a little nicer toward us. Maybe things would get better after all. I doubted it, but I hoped for the best.

A few weeks later things seemed as if they might turn around. I was playing in the driveway when Papa came home.

"Hey, Ronnie, go get Vic. I've got a surprise for you." I looked up from the rock castle I was building.

"Go on," he urged.

I jumped up and ran to the back door.

"Vic! C'mere!" I yelled through the screen door.

He came to the door after a few minutes. "What?"

He'd been inside watching cartoons and didn't want to come outside. Papa came to the porch.

"C'mon out, Vic. I want to show you boys something."

We followed Papa back down the driveway to his truck. The first glint of red metallic made us squeal with excitement. I hopped around anxiously. When he finally lifted the red tricycle and wagon from the truck, I felt breathless. Neither Vic nor I had ever received such a gift. Though there'd been plenty of bikes to ride at the home, this was something quite different. This was ours. We had no one else to share with. There was only the two of us.

Mama stood in the doorway and watched with mild amusement as we took turns riding back and forth across the pavement and into the gravel. We were a cloud of dust by the time we clamored into the house hours later.

For the first time since I can remember, it was dinnertime, but we weren't hungry. It was also the first time in weeks that we were happy enough not to think about leaving.

Unfortunately the feeling was short lived. I awoke early one morning with the hopes of getting on the tricycle first. Since I was so small, I had a hard time pedaling hard enough to pull the wagon. Because of that, Vic rarely let me ride. I figured if I got outside before him, I could practice riding.

Silently I got dressed and crept into the kitchen. There was a lingering smell of Papa's coffee in the air. He'd left for work long before the sun came up. I pushed the latch on the screen door and then went over to the corner of the washroom where the bike was standing. The wheels creaked softly as it rolled across the linoleum floor. I stopped right in front of the door and reached for the handle. I opened the door as far as I could and grabbed the handlebars. The door came swinging closed quickly and caught the bike at the pedals. It had not occurred to me that each time Vic and I rode the bike, one of us had held the door open while the other pushed everything onto the porch. Trying to do it alone was a struggle, but I didn't want to wake him. If I did, I wouldn't get a chance to ride.

I pushed the handlebars, but the bike was stuck. The pedal was lodged into the netting of the screen. The creaking of the floorboards in the hallway caught my attention. Someone was awake, probably Mama. I had to hurry and get outside. If I didn't, I'd get stuck doing chores. I tugged again at the bike, hard. In my elation over the success of getting outside, I'm not sure I even heard the screen ripping. The bike barreled onto the porch, and I hurriedly rolled it down the stairs and onto the driveway. I'd been riding for quite some time before Vic got up. He raced outside to find me covered in dust. I'd fallen over quite a few times, but I'd managed to master cycling well enough for us to take turns giving each other rides in the wagon.

By the time Mama's voice carried across the yard to call us inside, it was late into the morning. Her tone seemed especially cross, but neither of us attributed it to anything other than the fact that we'd snuck outside without doing our work. We trudged dirty and happy up the driveway to the porch, where she was waiting. The frown on her face and the gaping hole in the screen door stopped us in our tracks. My mouth dropped open.

"Look at what you've done!"

"Didn't do that," muttered Vic.

"Of course you did that," Mama yelled. "Get inside this house right now and go to your room!"

"No!" Vic screamed.

I turned and stared at him. He stood there with his arms folded defiantly. His reaction surprised me, but when Mama grabbed him by the arm and yanked him, I began to scream too.

"I-I-I did it," I stuttered. "It was an accident!" My admission didn't matter. She had already decided that she was angry with both of us. Vic kicked and screamed all the way to the bedroom and continued long after she left us there.

We soon tired and fell asleep. Sometime later, we were awakened by a vigorous shake. I raised my tear-stained face from the pillow and looked up to see Mrs. Booth standing over us, holding our jackets. I looked around and saw two black bags sitting on the floor by the door. What we had simultaneously wanted and feared was now happening. We were leaving.

Red Cross report dated March 31, 1951:

Worker feels this placement to be unsatisfactory. The children act out their hostilities, frequently, Victor more than Ronnie. Mrs. Siedeman is compulsive in her drive to control the children. Although warm, she is not understanding of the children's behavior and has little patience with them. She expects conformity to all her wishes; therefore, the children are a disappointment to her. At present she is willing to have the children leave for a new placement. During earlier visits Mrs. Siedeman could not permit herself this action as she has some guilt about her deficiencies. Today she blames the children for all troubles. Both children have reacted by being subtly destructive. They have marked walls and torn sheets. Victor will dawdle on his way to and from school. Mrs. Siedeman has been specific in setting a time limit for his return, but Victor is often late. Ronnie is more passive in his behavior and will make pitiful attempts to please his foster parents.

The children will be removed from this home as soon as a suitable home can be found. The parents have indicated their willingness to have the children returned to them. As soon as this possibility has been fully explored, a decision will be made. If this seems feasible the children will be returned. Both children have expressed their wish to be with their father and mother. Although the parents seem lacking in their ability to accept complete responsibility, it has been noted that they have much warmth and feelings for these children. Both Victor and Ron need the security of warm, emotional acceptance.

While I was doing the research on this book, I was able to contact all the foster parents and question them about our time with them. None of them knew that I had been able to get my hands on all the reports from the social workers and their reports to the social workers.

In her statement to me, Mrs. Siedeman said she remembered how she was able to break me out of the habit of dragging my left leg when I walked by forcing me to walk up and down a straight line for hours at a time. However, she neglected to have doctors check me out. If she had done this, she would have found that I had one leg longer than the other. Forcing me to walk in this manner has resulted in severe back problems. I have had six back surgeries since then.

Chapter Eight:
There's No Place like Home

MY FEELINGS WERE MIXED AS WE RODE AWAY FROM THE Siedemans'. I was happy that we were leaving. Living there had been more horrible than it had been fun. Mama's unpredictable mood swings and constant chastisement made it hard for my brother and me to relax.

But I was also sad.

Even though I liked the kids and the workers at the home, I wondered how long it would be before we'd get another chance at having a family.

I drifted off to sleep.

In my dreams, I imagined what the perfect parents would be like. I awoke with a smile on my face to the feel of soft hands tugging at my arm. When I opened my eyes, my smile faded.

Momma? Where were we?

I sat up quickly and looked around in shock. The faces of my mother and father beamed down at me. I looked over at Vic. We were back with our parents!

I climbed out of the car, my insides bubbling with uncertainty. I didn't know whether to be happy or sad. My father grabbed our bags from the car while Momma took us each by the hand.

I looked back at Mrs. Booth. She stood by the car door and waved at us. I waved back sadly, not sure I wanted to be there. I turned back around and looked at the house that stood in front of us. It was small, old, and weather beaten. The wooden shingles hung loosely from the roof, threatening to fall off at any moment. When we reached the porch, we stepped carefully over the holes in the steps.

The inside wasn't much better. The hardwood floor was dull and dusty. There was a small wooden table in the corner, with three wooden chairs. A fourth one stood off to the side, leaning against the wall due to a broken leg. There was a shabby brown sofa next to a matching chair that sat in front of a desolate looking fireplace. It was freezing outside, and equally cold inside.

"Welcome home, boys." Momma's voice was tentative, as if she wasn't really sure she meant what she'd just said. I looked over at Vic. He was taking in our new surroundings too. My father walked into another room with our bags.

"Boys," he called gruffly. We followed after him into a tiny room. There was a bookshelf in one corner and a dresser in the other and not much more.

"This is where you'll be sleeping."

Vic and I looked at him. There were no beds! Instead there was a pile of blankets on the floor off to the side of the bookcase.

Our father motioned toward them as if reading our minds.

"You'll spread those out and sleep on them. We'll get you something better a little later. When I can get some more work."

The emotionless tone of his voice chilled me more than the icy air around me.

"Me and your momma are going to get your brothers. You two unpack these bags and put your clothes away. We'll be back shortly. You understand?"

We both bobbed our heads.

Brothers?

I didn't know we had more than one. Did they mean Ralph Jr.? I was almost afraid to ask, but it didn't matter. Vic beat me to it.

"Do you mean little Ralph, sir?"

"Yeah," he answered shortly.

Without another word, he disappeared. We heard the front door open and shut, and then the sputtering of the old Buick that had been parked in the driveway.

Neither of us said a word as we unpacked our belongings, doing our best to shove everything into the limited drawer space. Finally we realized that it was impossible to get it all in, and we left some of our clothes in the bags.

"I'm hungry." My stomach had started growling on the long ride there since we hadn't been able to eat before leaving the Siedemans'.

In fact, they had barely looked at us as Mrs. Booth hustled us out the front door. It was almost as if they were pretending not to know us. I thought about Vic's wish not so long ago, to return to our mother and father. I wondered if he was happy.

"Are you glad we're back?" I asked him.

Vic shrugged.

"Don't know yet. Let's find something to eat."

We went back into the kitchen and looked around. A narrow white refrigerator stood in the corner. Vic went to it quickly and opened the door. The emptiness stared back at us. My stomach groaned anxiously. There was a bottle of milk on the door, a few brown eggs, and a stick of butter. Vic's face fell, full of disappointment. There was nothing for us to do but sit and wait.

Darkness fell and with it the room got colder. The house creaked under the blowing wind. Vic and I huddled on the floor of our room and grabbed the blankets to keep warm. It had been over two hours since our parents left. Along with the hunger in my stomach there sat a sinking feeling of being abandoned once more.

I was dozing off when the sound of the Buick's engine in the driveway woke me. The snap of the car doors jolted Vic awake, but neither of us moved. The front door opened and closed, and immediately the sound of a baby's cry filled the house.

Ralph!

I jumped up and ran into the other room to see my little brother but stopped short. There were two babies.

Wide eyed, I looked from one to the other. It wasn't hard to tell which one was Ralph, but who was this other baby?

"This is your brother, Simon," Momma said as she moved toward us.

I looked at him. He was tiny, bundled up in several blankets. He reminded me of the way Ralph looked the day that we'd been taken away over a year ago.

"Hello, Simon," Vic said solemnly as he looked down on our new brother. Then he turned cheerfully to Ralph. "Hi, Ralph."

Ralph was a toddler and wobbly on his legs. He stood near Momma. When Vic spoke to him, he looked in our direction. He looked from Vic to me and began to cry. He didn't recognize us. He turned back to Momma and clutched her leg. She picked him up and cooed at him, rocking him into silence. For a moment, I wished I was him.

Dinner was a scant helping of beans and a glass of milk. I received a stern glare when I asked for seconds and realized quickly that there wasn't any more to be had. My stomach groaned its protest in the middle of the night as Vic and I lay in our blankets on the floor. Sleep was a long time coming.

It didn't take long for Ralph to get to know us. After a few days he wobbled to us whenever he saw us. Though we were delighted by this recognition, with it came the responsibility of watching his every move.

Every morning started out the same. My father left well before the sun came up, before any of us were awake. Vic and I awakened to the sounds of Simon's cries. Momma hustled around fixing his bottle and getting him dressed. We scurried around fetching diapers and other things that she asked us for. She fixed a quick breakfast, usually consisting of toast and cheese with a glass of milk. The amount of food was never enough, but we were not permitted to say so. We were too scared to ask for more.

A couple of weeks after our arrival, my parents decided that they could not afford to leave Ralph at the sitter any longer. That was when Momma began leaving him at home with us.

"Keep an eye on your brother," she would say as she walked out the door with Simon in her arms. It was hard to amuse Ralph. We didn't have anything to play with except the small army men that we'd brought with us. Momma had already told us that we could not let Ralph play with them, because he could swallow them, so we were forced to find other ways to keep him from crying.

One evening while we were waiting for Momma to come home, Ralph would not be quiet. It was later than usual, and he had already drunk all his bottles. The house was cold and we sat shivering.

"Let's make a fire," said Vic.

I stared at him. "With what?"

We'd barely seen our father make a fire, let alone ever made one ourselves. Father had always told us that we were too little to make the fire, although we weren't too little to carry the heavy bundles of wood. Ralph was still wailing, and I wondered what making a fire would do about making him get quiet.

"Shhh, Ralph. Don't cry," I said pleadingly.

I watched as Vic walked over to the fireplace and picked up a piece of kindling from the stack of wood. When he found a piece that he liked, he took it over to the stove. Next he turned the knob on the stove. The hissing sound of the gas filled the air.

I looked at him with surprise. "Oooh, Vic! You're not supposed to do that! We're going to get into trouble!"

"It's cold," he said. "We have to stop Ralph from being cold." He found the matches and struck one. Nothing happened. The pungent smell of gas continued to fill the room. Vic tried to light another match and again nothing happened.

"Turn it off, Vic," I whined.

"Don't you start crying, too," he said.

I sniffed loudly and poked out my lip, angry that he had implied that I was going to be a crybaby like our little brother.

Vic struck the match again and it sparked. The fire spread as he put the match to the burner as we'd seen Momma do many times. I watched in awe, scarcely aware that Ralph had become quiet at the sight of the glowing fire. It wasn't until he squealed with delight that I paid attention to him again. Both of us were watching Vic. Just as he stuck the kindling in the fire, Momma walked in.

"What is going on in here?" Her voice startled us all.

I jumped, Ralph began to wail, and Vic dropped the kindling on the floor. The fire quickly consumed the small piece of wood and searched for something to keep it alive. It found a nearby scant rug and began to blaze.

Momma dropped the bag in her arm, set Simon down, and rushed over to the growing fire. She jumped up and down, stomping furiously on the rug, trying to squelch the fire. All of us stood still and watched her with our mouths open.

We didn't hear my father come in. Without a word, he rushed over and began stomping on the fire alongside Momma.

Finally they were able to put it out. Ashes covered the area, and there was a cloud of smoke that floated around the room. A black scorch mark marred the floor. Simon started crying, and Ralph began coughing from the smoke. Momma ran to attend to them. My father turned on us, his eyes holding a fire of their own.

"Thought I told you boys not to mess with the fire."

"B-b-but it was cold, sir." Vic was trembling slightly.

"You disobeyed me, boy. Ronnie, go run and get a switch."

I was stuck in my place. Though both our parents had threatened to whip us several times since our arrival, they had, until now, not laid a hand on us. I didn't even know what a switch was!

"I said move, boy!"

I began to cry but still didn't move. I couldn't. I didn't know what to do. Taking my actions as disobedience, my father stormed past us and out the front door. He grabbed a small branch from the tree in front of our house and returned to the house. Vic's eyes widened as father came toward him holding the switch.

Swat!

Vic howled with pain as my father smacked him on the backside several times.

"Don't ... ever ... disobey ... me again!"

A swat followed as he broke down each syllable of his sentence. He let go of Vic's arm and moved toward me. I moved backward in fear, but he reached out and pulled me to him.

"And you," he breathed heavily. "When I tell you to do something, you do it!"

He swatted me three quick times and let go. We were sent to our room, our behinds stinging and our pride hurt. We lay down on our blankets sniffling, eventually drifting off to sleep.

During the weeks that followed that incident, it seemed that Vic and I were the only ones getting thinner. Both

Simon and Ralph always had enough to eat. Momma often commented that people donated the formula for the babies. I wished we were so lucky. The nights were that much longer with nothing in our stomachs. The cheese sandwiches that were left for our lunch did not calm the growing pangs of hunger. Each night I wished Mrs. Booth would come back and take us. It didn't matter where we went, as long as we left the place we were in.

Chapter Nine:
Holiday Hell

CHRISTMAS WAS COMING AROUND AGAIN, BUT THERE WERE NONE of the festivities that we'd experienced at Covenant. The weather turned bitingly cold, and we spent most days huddled under our blankets with Ralph, waiting for our parents to come home and start a fire.

One morning, about a week before Christmas, we woke up late. The house was unusually quiet. I got up and scurried across the cold floor to the kitchen.

No one was there, and things seemed different.

The familiar smell of my father's coffee didn't fill the room. I raced to the window and looked outside. Our old Buick was still parked in the driveway. That meant our father was still home. I went back to the room and burrowed back under the covers. I decided to wait there until Momma made us get up. If my father were still home, maybe we would all be home together.

I drifted back to sleep. Momma rushed into our room and woke us. Her face was stained with tears, but she appeared to be angry with us.

"Get up and watch your brother!" she growled at us, and plunked Ralph down on my legs. She disappeared quickly, and I listened as she moved around in the kitchen getting Simon ready. Her sniffles carried into our room, and I got up to see what was the matter.

"Momma?" She turned on me, and I saw the tears running down her face. I had never seen her cry before.

"What's the matter, Momma? Where's Daddy?"

She dropped the baby bottle that she'd been holding. Formula splattered onto the floor. Some of the warm milk hit my bare foot and I jumped. Momma glared at me through the tears in her eyes.

"Shut your mouth!" she screamed. Vic ran into the room, curious about the commotion.

"What's wrong?" he asked. Though he was asking me, his question infuriated Momma more.

"Your father left!" she spat.

"But the car ..." I began. I was confused. Why was she mad that he left?

He left every morning, didn't he? "He left and he isn't coming back!" It took a moment for that to sink in. Where had he gone? Why had he left?

Vic voiced my thoughts.

"Why, Momma?" His question was innocent, but the resentment in Momma's eyes flashed angrily. Her words were equally as venomous.

"He left coz of you two!" She turned, picked up Simon, and walked out the door.

The Buick fired up and sputtered out of the driveway. She'd left us alone with no breakfast. My heart sank as I thought about my mother's words. I tried to think of what we had done to make our father leave. I concluded that it was because we were bad kids. After the spanking over the fire we received them somewhat regularly. My father was always angry with us.

We waited until well after dark for our mother to come home. Ralph had long since run out of bottles, and so we gave him regular milk from the refrigerator. It didn't sit well in his stomach and gave him diarrhea. The house smelled of sour diapers. When Momma came in, we cringed, expecting her to yell at any moment.

Instead, she staggered past us into her bedroom and closed the door. We both looked at each other.

Where was Simon?

When it became apparent that she wasn't coming out again, we gave Ralph another regular milk bottle and went to bed hungry.

Our days and nights continued in about that fashion for almost a week. Some days Momma remembered to leave us something, but most times she acted as if we weren't there. She left early in the morning and came in very late at night. We hadn't seen Simon in a long time, but neither of us was willing to risk setting off Momma's temper by asking where he was. It was no surprise when Mrs. Booth returned one morning and picked us up. Again there was another woman with her, and she took Ralph away in a separate car. We rode for several hours before stopping.

Mrs. Booth fed us hamburgers and French fries. She even treated us to milkshakes! Vic and I savored the taste of the cold, creamy treat on our tongues. We rode for a few more hours into a rural area, passing several large fields with cows, goats, and horses. Vic and I looked out the window at all the animals in amazement. We'd never seen so many of them in one place. We made a game out of trying to see who could count the most of each type of animal. We'd become so engrossed that we didn't even notice the house until we stopped.

The gravel driveway was long and winding and led up to a tall two-story house with gray siding. Just beyond the house was a red barn. The paint was peeling and weathered from enduring many winter rains. On the right there was a small brown shack. It was impossible to imagine anybody living in something so tiny. The land sprawled out for what seemed like forever. There was a gate on the left of us where a bunch of cows were grazing.

Even though Mrs. Booth had told us to stay put, we jumped out of the car and ran over to the fence, peeping through the slats at the cows. They ignored us and continued chewing on the grass. I reached between the slats in the fence. I wanted to touch them. I'd never been that close to any animal other than a dog, but they were not willing to cooperate and remained just out of my reach.

Disappointed, I moved from the fence and kicked rocks up the driveway. The squawk of some wandering chickens caught our attention.

At the far end of the field was a long, narrow, white chicken house. There were bunches of chickens strutting around, stopping occasionally to scratch and peck at the ground. Vic and I ran to the other side of the gate and squatted down to watch them, fascinated.

Where are we?

The sound of a screen door banging closed, followed by women's voices, caught my attention. I looked up the road and saw Mrs. Booth talking to a woman. Vic looked at me, and we crept quietly closer to the door so that we could hear.

"Look, Mrs. Booth," the woman said, "I told the agency that we only wanted to take in girls. Boys are much too difficult to raise."

Mrs. Booth glanced around the land. "Mrs. Borg, surely you can understand my situation. These young boys have had a difficult time, but I can assure you that they will not be any trouble to you. They really need a home."

We held our breath and waited while Mrs. Borg stood quietly contemplating what Mrs. Booth had just said. Silently we willed her to say yes. As far as we could tell, this place was wonderful. Besides, we worried that if she did not take us in, Mrs. Booth would be forced to take us back to our mother.

Mrs. Borg sighed loudly. "All right, they can stay. But if I have one lick of trouble from them, I'm going to call you to come back for them."

"Of course," Mrs. Booth agreed. She turned in the direction of the car.

"Vic, Ronnie," she called out to us. We jumped out from our hiding place and ran toward her. She frowned at our disobedience for not having stayed in the car but didn't say anything.

"Boys, this is Mrs. Borg. You'll be staying here with her and her husband."

Upon getting a closer look, neither Vic nor I was sure what to make of Mrs. Borg. She was a short, portly woman wearing a yellow housedress with an apron. She stared down at us with eyes that didn't have a smile hidden anywhere in them. Nothing about her appearance welcomed us.

My voice left my throat, until Mrs. Booth nudged us.

"Hello, ma'am," we both said shyly.

She looked each of us over, drawing us to her, checking our hair, ears, and even inside our mouths, as if she were inspecting a puppy. Finally she said "hello." Her voice was gruff and uninviting. I began to think that staying there would not be such a wonderful idea after all. But it was settled. Mrs. Borg would take us in, provided we didn't cause any trouble.

As far as I could tell, we never did, but like most anything else, that was a matter of opinion.

And so, for the third time in less than three years, Vic and I stood at the end of a road, waving good-bye to Mrs. Booth in her black sedan. For the third time, we had no idea what we were in for. For the millionth time, I was scared.

Chapter Ten:
A Confusion of Manners

IF WE'D BEEN UNSURE OF HOW TO READ MRS. BORG UPON MEETING her, Mr. Borg made things crystal clear. His old, beat-up Ford barreled down the gravel driveway, heaped with bags of sod, grain, and other items from the feed store in town.

Vic and I had been sitting on the porch. After Mrs. Booth left, we hadn't known what to do. Mrs. Borg didn't invite us into the house. She'd stood on the porch and watched the sedan disappear, then looked at us with disdain and returned inside the house.

When Mr. Borg got out of the truck, our eyes widened. He was a tall, heavyset man, with thick, bushy eyebrows and a permanent scowl on his face. We watched as he grabbed a sack of feed from the bed of the truck and slung it over his massive shoulders. He walked over to the weather-beaten barn and disappeared inside. After several trips, he looked over at us.

"Who are you?" His gruff voice made me so nervous that I started to shake. "Well?" he boomed impatiently.

Mrs. Borg came to the screen door. "Agency brought 'em," she said flatly. "Told 'em we wanted girls, but she says these here boys were all she had. Didn't have nowhere else for 'em."

Mr. Borg looked us over and grunted. "Well, what are your names?"

"I'm Vic," my brother answered. "This is Ronnie," he said, when I didn't answer after a few seconds.

He looked us over again, grunted, and headed back toward the truck. He shouldered another sack of feed and then looked in our direction.

"If you're going to live here, you'll earn your keep. When I come home with a load, you'll pitch in until we're done."

We stood up but remained frozen to our spots. We weren't quite sure what he wanted us to do. When we didn't move, Mr. Borg's scowl deepened.

"Get over here and grab a sack of feed. Now!" The thunder in his voice lifted the glue on the bottoms of our feet. Vic and I scrambled over to the truck.

"Hold your arms out," he said. We did as we were told. Mr. Borg dropped a sack onto our waiting arms. The heavy load staggered us, and we tumbled to the ground. I started to cry.

"Quit that sissy crying!" he bellowed.

He bent down and grabbed the sack.

"Hold your arms out."

I sniffled loudly, got to my feet, and held my arms out as I'd been told. Mr. Borg dropped the sack onto us again with the same amount of force as before. We staggered and fell again but got quickly to our feet.

After several more failed attempts, Mr. Borg decided to give us smaller sacks to carry. We managed to carry half and half drag those sacks to the barn and stack them as we were instructed. We worked for over two hours before finally trudging into the house. We were covered in dirt, and my arms and legs burned.

When we got inside, Mr. Borg disappeared. Since it was our very first time inside the house, we had no idea where to go, so we stood in the middle of the front hallway and waited. The smell of fried pork chops drifted under my nose and my stomach lurched. It had been hours since we'd eaten, but after what we had gone through with our parents, it felt more like days.

Several minutes passed before Mrs. Borg stepped out of the kitchen and noticed us standing there.

"Well for goodness' sake, get yourselves up there and get cleaned up!"

Our legs moved heavily up the stairs in the direction that her arm pointed. It was dark, and we had no idea which way to go. I followed Vic to the left and by luck we found the bathroom at the end of the dark hallway. Vic felt around the wall in search of a light switch, but there was none, so we went to the sink and did the best we could in the dark. When we finished we wiped our hands on our dirty pants, which defeated the purpose of washing altogether.

As we exited the bathroom, Mr. Borg stepped out of a tiny room. His size intimidated us once more as he loomed over us and we stood still. He frowned, stepped around us, and disappeared again into the bathroom. We looked at each other and then hurried back down the stairs toward the only light we saw.

The kitchen was small and dingy. An old refrigerator hissed in the corner, as if it was about to conk out at any moment.

The paint on the white cabinets was peeling, and the floor linoleum had curled up around the edges. A small table stood at the far end underneath a drawstring light. Mrs. Borg was standing over the stove with her fork in a pan of hot grease. Her back was to us.

We stood there for a few moments, waiting for her to turn around. When she didn't, Vic spoke up. "Excuse me, ma'am. What do you want us to do now?"

The sound of Vic's tiny voice startled Mrs. Borg, and she then whirled around with a scowl.

"Don't ya' ever come sneaking up on me again! Do ya' hear me?"

We both nodded vigorously. Vic bit his lip to keep from crying. Seeing our faces, she softened a bit and pointed toward the table.

"Go on over there and sit down. Mister will be in here in a minute and you all can eat."

We scrambled over to the table and sat down. Mr. Borg came and sat down a few minutes later. Again he frowned at us, but didn't say a word. Mrs. Borg brought over plates of pork chops, rice, and cabbage and sat them in front of us. When she sat down, Vic and I waited expectantly. At the Siedemans' we'd been taught to wait until Papa began eating before we ate. We weren't sure if the same thing applied here, but we didn't want to run the risk of being scolded again.

"Something wrong that you can't eat my food?" Mrs. Borg stared at us.

She had already begun to eat her food, but Mr. Borg sat looking at us.

"No, ma'am," we both whispered.

A few more moments passed, and she looked our way again. Neither of us had moved, although both of our stomachs were rumbling ferociously. The clanging sound of Mrs. Borg dropping her fork against her plate made me jump. She was clearly angry with us.

"Start eating, now, or else I'll just take those plates from you. Go to bed hungry for all I care!"

She continued to mutter under her breath about us being ungrateful and how she'd told those people that she didn't want boys anyhow. My heart was racing in my chest. I certainly didn't want her taking my plate, but when I stole a glance at Mr. Borg, he hadn't moved. He was still looking us over, as if he was trying to figure out something about us.

"All right, that's it!" I gasped when I saw her get up and reach for our plates. Vic's eyes widened. The idea of going to bed without eating was suddenly about to become a reality.

Why did it seem that we were always being punished?

"Leave 'em alone, Ruth!" Mr. Borg's voice bellowed into the silence, quickening my heartbeat even more. Mrs. Borg stopped in her tracks and stared at her husband. By the expression on her face, it was obvious that she didn't take too kindly to the tone he had taken with her in front of us, but it was equally obvious that he didn't care.

"Look at me," he commanded.

Both Vic and I did as we were told. I felt a chill in my body, and I trembled slightly.

"You boys been taught not to touch your food 'til the man of the table eats, that right?"

We nodded our heads vigorously. I felt the air sail out of my body in relief. Thank God he understood!

"What kind of nonsense ..."

"Hush, Ruth," he interrupted her before she could finish. "Good to know you boys been taught right," he said.

His face softened some, but I wouldn't have called what he did a smile. He picked up his fork and scooped some rice into his mouth. I happily followed suit, while Vic opted to dig right into his pork chop. Mrs. Borg looked from one to the other of us before finally sitting back down. Not another word was said at the table, and that suited me just fine.

Chapter Eleven:
Punishment

IN TAKE STUDY
RONALD EUGENE SOMMERVILLE (B. 2-6-46)
Foster parents:
Arthur and Lillian Borg
RR #1, Box 231
Frankfort, Illinois
BEHAVIOR

Early childhood symptoms of disturbances such as enuresis, stealing, tantrums, passive withdrawing, and non conformity have subsided considerably in submerged repressive and suppressive states. Light volcanic eruptions, disturbances occur occasionally when uncontrolled devices break down from an overloading of the withdrawal and withholding mechanisms. Ronald will reverse his mechanistic operating defenses and reveal part of his basic self and feelings by becoming aggressively hostile and demanding. The action taken may be directed at self by further withdrawal and self pity or at others by exhibiting his temper. On several occasions during these states he has threatened to run away from his foster home (hence, getting back at his foster mother). On fewer occasions he has actually carried out his threat by running away to the farm boundary lines. (Not noted in the report was that, "I ran about ten miles away because Victor and I were forced to kneel on bricks in the hot sun with bare knees for a long period of time." Another time Ron ran away, which is also not in this report, was when Mrs. Borg tried to force Victor and Ronald's hands in a fire which she started in a pan because they were playing with matches. None of this information will be found in these reports because the social worker refused to believe Victor and Ronald.) Lack of sympathy and understanding from his foster mother regarding his running away has thwarted and confused Ronald so that he is left in a quandary as to how to release his cumulated, explosive, indulging in self pity. Accompanying this cathartic release is the renewed building up of a hard resistive-proof shell to withstand further "attacks" of rejection by his foster mother. The above descriptive information reveals that Ronald's main defense producing fear is one of rejection. Unfortunately, Mrs. Borg's personality structure makes it difficult for Ronald to receive the love, affection, and attention he needs. She is masculinely inclined and feels more comfortable with a child who is the rough and tough type. Interpretively speaking, she is not prepared because of a lacking in her early life, to give love and affection. Ronald's earlier bids for love and affection were interpreted by Mrs. Borg as being sissified and effeminate. She, therefore, used to "shoo" him outside to rough and tough it with Victor. Instead of love and attention, Ronald received rejection.

"Ouch!"

My startled cry caused Vic to jump straight up in bed and with good reason. When he looked over to where I was laying, he saw a huge crow pecking at my toes through the covers. My eyes widened with terror as I squirmed away from the flutter of its wings and the sharp peck of its beak.

Where had this mad bird come from?

"Shoo!" Vic ran over and flailed his arms at the bird, hoping to make it go away, but the bird kept hovering around me, squawking every so often as if taunting me. It was obvious that the enormous bird was not intimidated by Vic's feeble shouts, so my brother picked up a shoe that was near the bed. Just as he was about to hurl it, Mrs. Borg came in.

"All right, Nicodemus, let 'em alone." And just like that, the bird flew away from us and landed on Mrs. Borg's shoulder. Both Vic and I stared at her, our mouths hanging wide open.

"Boy, put that shoe down. Don't 'cha be throwing things at ol' Nicodemus. I sent him in here to wake you two lazy things up!"

The shoe dropped to the floor with a thud, but still neither of us moved or said a word. Not only was the bird Mrs. Borg's, but she'd sent it in our room to wake us up. That was definitely something new to us.

"Well don't just stand there! Get your clothes on and come on in here if you wanna eat breakfast! Got chores to do today!" She turned, the bird still on her shoulder, and walked downstairs to the kitchen.

For about half a second, we just stood there. I had gotten over being scared and was now pretty amazed by the trained bird. I chuckled a little. The nips hadn't really hurt, but it had surely surprised the daylights out of me. I grabbed a pair of pants and a shirt from the small wooden dresser that held our clothes and dressed hurriedly. When we reached the kitchen, Mrs. Borg had placed two steaming bowls of oatmeal on the table along with two glasses of milk. Since ours were the only dishes on the table, we felt safe in assuming that Mr. Borg would not be sitting down with us. Mrs. Borg was nowhere in sight, but we could hear Nicodemus squawking outside on the porch, so we figured she was close by.

The two of us ate quickly and quietly, making sure to clean up after ourselves once we finished. When we stepped out onto the porch, Mrs. Borg was waiting for us.

"'Bout time you two got out here. C'mon now so we can get started afore Mister gets upset."

She stepped down onto the soft dirt road and walked toward the barn. Out of nowhere, Nicodemus swooped down and perched onto her shoulder.

"Rover, Jenny, get on over here," she called.

Neither Vic nor I had a clue who Rover or Jenny were, until two dogs came bounding over from behind the house. Mrs. Borg stopped when the dogs reached her.

"Sit down, you mangy things!" The two animals immediately obeyed her and looked up expectantly for the next command. She beckoned both of us over to where she was standing.

"This here's Rover," she said, pointing to a skinny brown Newfoundland. "And this one here is Jenny."

Jenny, a red and white Collie, wagged her tail vigorously as Mrs. Borg patted her on the head. I inched over to the dogs but stopped when Rover tensed up.

"Take your time, boy. Rover doesn't like folks too much he don't know."

I stood there for a moment and decided to approach Jenny first. She seemed to be a little friendlier. I rubbed her head, and she responded by licking me playfully. I looked behind me and saw my brother still standing in the same spot.

"C'mon, Vic. She's nice." I moved over so that he could stand next to me.

Mrs. Borg watched us and so did Rover.

After a while I think he got jealous, because he came over and nudged his way in between us so that he could get some of our attention. I laughed as his warm tongue tickled across my fingers.

"All right, that's enough," Mrs. Borg said gruffly. She turned and trudged ahead toward the barn. As if they understood her words, both Jenny and Rover tagged along behind.

There was nothing left for Vic and I to do but follow as well. It had been too dark, and we'd been too nervous the night before, to pay much attention to the inside of the barn. But as we stood in the middle of it in the early morning hours, we noticed the sweet smelling bales of hay stacked on one side.

There was an old, yellow tractor parked near the window, and several tools. In the corner were the bags of feed that we'd helped Mr. Borg carry in. There were three stalls, although no horses were inside. Mrs. Borg paused a moment to let us look around before getting down to the business of chores.

"Grab one of them pails over there. Both of you."

We followed the direction of her extended finger to a corner of the barn near the door, where there were several metal pails stacked inside each other. Vic took one and handed me another, and we rushed back to her side, awaiting her next instruction. It was kind of exciting, since neither of us had ever been in a place so big, with so many animals.

"See those barrels right there?" she asked, pointing again but in a different direction. We nodded once we spotted the weathered, wooden barrels.

"Open one of 'em up and scoop some of that feed in both of them pails."

Vic and I looked at each other and then took off in a race to see who could get there first. He beat me by a half a second and slid the lid off of the first barrel he came to. We stood on our tiptoes and peeked inside.

The barrel was half full with a mixture of corn and grain and a large metal scoop. Since Vic got there first, it meant that he would get to be the one to scoop the feed while I held the pail. The only problem was that the barrel was tall and the feed was low inside.

He stared into the barrel, then tried to stretch his arm to reach the metal scoop. But of course, he couldn't. Vic thought for a moment.

While I waited, I stole a glance over at Mrs. Borg, who was busying herself with something on a shelf behind one of the stalls. Silently I willed Vic to hurry up with an idea. Something told me that if Mrs. Borg became impatient, it could easily erupt into anger.

"Ronnie, lay that pail down."

I looked quizzically at my brother.

Lay it down?

I had no idea what he was talking about. Reading the confusion in my face, he grabbed the pail from my hands and laid it on the ground upside down.

"Oh," I said, as I finally understood what he was doing. With the pail on the ground he now had a stepping stool that allowed him to reach down far enough into the barrel. Vic scooped feed into the pail. I watched as the mixture of corn slid off the scoop and into the pail with a clanging sound. It had a strong, sweet smell, and I wondered what made this corn different from the kind we ate at dinnertime.

Once the pail was full, I sat it down on the ground and raced over to get another empty one. Mrs. Borg looked over at me when I breezed by, and I could feel her eyes watching me as I grabbed another pail and ran back to where Vic was.

Please don't let her get angry, I thought as I held the pail for my brother.

"Hurry up, Vic," I whispered. He was about to protest, but he seemed to think better of it after looking over his shoulder and seeing that we were being watched. He shoveled faster, and when he finished, I sat the pail next to the first one. Vic carefully replaced the lid on the barrel while I returned the empty pail.

Mrs. Borg was still looking at us, but her expression didn't appear angry. In fact, it was probably the closest thing to a smile we'd seen from her so far. We lugged the full buckets of feed over to where she was standing, but before we could put them down, she turned and walked out of the barn.

"Let's go," she called over her shoulder. We followed her around the side of the barn over to the small brown shack we'd noticed the day before. As we got closer, I could hear faint clucking sounds, growing louder. It was a hen house. Mrs. Borg swung the door open. We were about to step inside when she stopped us.

"Stop right here. You go in there with them full pails and them hens gonna swarm all over ya."

She reached in my pail and took a fistful of feed. "Stay here. When they come out, take your hand and start scattering it on the ground out here."

She disappeared and then reappeared shortly thereafter, a bunch of hens strutting out behind her. We watched as she sprinkled a bit of the corn, and the birds anxiously pecked it up as soon as it hit the ground.

"Go on and get started," she said.

Holding the pail by the handle and the bottom, I began shaking feed onto the ground. Vic did the same.

"Not like that!" she shouted, gruffly. "Use your hand like you saw me do. And don't stand so close together. Spread out some, else you gonna have a fight on your hands!"

I went left, while Vic went right, sprinkling food out the way we'd seen Mrs. Borg do it. Before I knew it, there were hens and roosters everywhere. There were red ones, white ones, and black ones. In all, I think there must have been about fifty of them. When the pails were empty we stood there and watched the birds scratch and peck at the ground. The roosters strutted around, not really eating as much as putting on a show for the hens around them.

"Let's go," she called. "We ain't got all morning!"

Vic turned to follow her into the hen house, but I was still stuck watching the bevy of birds in front of me.

"Ronnie! C'mon!" Vic came back and tugged me by the arm into the hen house. Inside the hen house were several rows of nests. The floor was covered in hay, and stray feathers were scattered here and there. Mrs. Borg had already made her way to the first row of nests. She had a large basket in her hand.

"Get some of that hay over there." She pointed to a broken up bale of hay near the door. Vic and I did as we were told. I inhaled the sweetness of the hay as I grabbed a fistful.

"Put it in the bottom of your buckets like this." She held up her already lined basket to show us, and we copied what we saw. Next, she reached into one of the nests and pulled out two eggs. Both of our eyes widened like saucers. We'd never seen eggs come from anywhere other than a store.

"Well don't just stand there." Both of us ran to a row of nests and began reaching inside. The eggs felt warm, and that too was a surprise to me. I looked across at Vic, and he seemed to be having a good time doing this new chore. We each finished our rows and moved on to the next.

Fifteen minutes later we were carrying our nearly full buckets into the house. Although they weren't very heavy, it was a chore to keep them from rolling around so they wouldn't crack. Rover and Jenny darting around and in between us made it that much more difficult.

When we got to the house, Mrs. Borg told us to set them on top of the kitchen table, while she went to get a bowl of water.

"Ronnie, you dip 'em in the water and Vic's gonna dry 'em," she said, passing him a small towel.

She had also come back with two very large empty bowls, which she said were for the eggs once they were washed. I took an egg, carefully dipped it in the water, and then passed it to Vic. And then I did another. By about the fourth egg, Mrs. Borg bellowed at us about moving too slow. The impatience in her voice made me so nervous that the next three eggs I dipped slipped through my fingers and cracked. This, of course, only made her mad, and she fussed the whole time that she was at the sink changing the water.

Over the next few weeks we settled into a routine on the Borgs' farm. After our first full day of chores, Mrs. Borg added several others that kept us occupied from six in the morning well into the twilight hours. Most days she watched us for the first couple of hours and then disappeared into the house to do her cleaning. As soon as she left us, Vic and I usually found ways to amuse ourselves in between feeding animals, collecting milk and eggs and pulling weeds in Mrs. Borg's small garden.

We spent a lot of time in the barn. In fact, it was our favorite place, because there were so many spots to hide in. It was like our secret clubhouse, except it wasn't really a secret.

Neither Vic nor I were fond of chores to begin with— cleaning the pigpen was probably the thing we hated the most. It seemed as though the area was always muddy, and it was often hard to tell the difference between the wet earth and the manure that we were supposed to clean up. Because of this, we were constantly cleaning our raggedy tennis shoes to rid them of the stench that lingered behind us.

We were in the midst of cleaning our shoes one afternoon when Vic suddenly had to go to the bathroom. I wasn't sure what was wrong with him, but he had been having a terrible stomachache all day and had made several trips to the outhouse already. When he bolted from the bale of hay that we were sitting on and took off running, I knew where he was headed. Even though I felt bad for him I couldn't help but chuckle. I mean, it was a little funny.

I was still scraping my shoe with a stick when I heard my name being called in the distance. I jumped up and ran around the side of the barn toward the porch. I was almost there when I heard the muffled voice again. It was Vic, calling me from the outhouse. I ran toward the sound of his voice and stopped outside the door.

"I'm right here," I answered, when he called me again. "What is it, Vic?"

"There's no paper in here for me to wipe," he said. "Can you go get some?"

I suppressed a laugh. The idea of Vic stuck with no toilet paper was indeed funny. If I'd wanted to be mean, I could leave and just let him stay in there. But then I thought better of it. I knew how bad the smell could get in there, and since he'd been running in there all day I figured he could really be sick. My leaving him stranded like that wouldn't be nice. Besides, Vic was always really good about coming with me when I needed to go in the middle of the night.

"I'll be right back," I called back to him. I dashed off to the house, flung open the screen door to the porch, and hurried to the cabinet in the hallway. I was pulling a roll of the stiff paper from its package when Mrs. Borg came up behind me.

"What are you doing in my house?"

I hadn't heard her coming, and the sound of her voice right behind me startled the daylights out of me. I fell over from my crouched position but jumped up quickly. She was glaring down at me, and my words got stuck in my throat, as they always seemed to do when I stood before her.

"How many times I tell y'all to stay out of my house? You don't come in here until I call ya!" Her face was reddening, an obvious sign that her anger was almost at a boil.

"Y-y-yes, ma'am, b-b-but, my b-b-brother," I began.

She cut me off before I could finish. "Look at this mess you've made!"

She yanked me from the closet and pointed to the dirty tracks on the hardwood floor. My mouth gaped open. I'd forgotten that my shoes were still covered from the pigpen.

"I-I-I'm s-s-sorry, ma'am."

That dreaded stutter of mine was getting worse with each passing moment. I wanted to tell her why I'd come inside, though I knew she wouldn't care. I had to tell her about Vic, but my tongue felt as if it had doubled in size. The words would never come out right, and the more I stuttered, the angrier Mrs. Borg became.

"Hush your mouth with all that babbling!" she screamed. "Told that damn agency woman I didn't want no boys around here. Certainly didn't want any dummies."

Her comment stung. It wasn't as if that was the first time she'd called me dumb. In fact, she said it quite frequently. That still didn't stop it from hurting my feelings.

"B-b-but, Vic," I stammered. My face grew flustered as tears welled up in my eyes. Unfortunately, crying was another weakness Mrs. Borg preyed upon.

"Not only are ya dumb, but you're a sissy too! Lord, why me?"

She looked up in the sky as if expecting an answer from the Lord at any moment. I contemplated making a run for it. I didn't want to leave Vic stranded in the outhouse. I figured I was going to get whipped anyhow, so what did I have to lose?

I took a deep breath, swallowing the emotion that was threatening to spill over. Mrs. Borg was still ranting at me, but her grip on my arm had loosened. I looked back into the cabinet at the roll of toilet paper that I'd managed to unwrap. If I were going to make a break for it, I'd have to be fast.

With one swift motion, I snatched my arm from Mrs. Borg's grasp, grabbed the toilet paper roll, dashed around the angry woman, and burst through the door. My heart was pumping as fast as the little legs that carried me to the outhouse. It wasn't as though I thought Mrs. Borg would chase me, but my fear over what I had just done prevented me from slowing down after I'd broke free of her.

"Vic," I called breathlessly, once I was outside the door. He opened the door just enough for me to hand him the roll of paper.

"Thanks," he said, after the door slammed shut again.

I fell to the ground, still trying to catch my breath. I glanced expectantly at the porch and was not surprised to find Mrs. Borg standing there. The weight of her glare was like an anvil. Her arms were folded, and it wasn't hard to guess that she was waiting for me to come back. I sat there a moment longer wondering how much worse the whipping would be the longer I waited. Mrs. Borg could be extremely heavy handed when it came to whipping us. A mere switch felt more like a heavy plank smacking down on our behinds.

Reluctantly, I stood up. While I didn't relish the thought of the punishment to come, I didn't want to risk not eating today.

It was only noon, and while I was sure that I had run my way out of lunch, I figured I could still get dinner if I took my beating now. I was just reaching the porch steps when I heard the outhouse door slam behind me. I looked over my shoulder and saw Vic walking out. His mouth dropped open when he saw Mrs. Borg standing on the porch. I turned away from him, only to find that Mrs. Borg was now right in front of me.

"You got nerve enough to pull away from me, huh, boy? First ya dirty up my clean house, and then ya wanna get mannish and leave while I'm talking to ya! Well, I've got something for you, ya ungrateful little—"

"Wait," Vic interrupted. He'd run over to plead my case.

"There wasn't any paper in the outhouse, ma'am. Ronnie was just bringing me some, coz my stomach's been hurting awfully bad."

"Shut up!" she yelled at him. "If I wanna hear something from you, I'll ask you! That's the trouble with you two, always mouthing off. You'd better get away from here boy, and get back to your chores unless you want some of this switch too!"

Vic opened his mouth but then thought better of it. I could tell he didn't know what to do. Normally the threat of a whipping didn't scare him, but I imagine his backside was sore enough from all those trips to the bathroom. He gave me a sad look, as if to apologize, then turned toward the barn. Mrs. Borg pulled me to the porch. Next to the hand pump was the switch that she used to whip us all the time. She grabbed it and yanked at my pants. When she'd exposed my bare bottom, she swatted me repeatedly.

"Teach you to defy me," she exclaimed, as the wiry branch smacked against my butt. I hollered in pain with each swat.

Tears streamed down my face. It felt as though she would never stop, and I wondered for the millionth time why she hated us so much. I'd only been trying to help my brother. Why couldn't she see that? Wouldn't it have been enough to make me clean up the mess I'd made?

Finally the blows stopped coming, and she released her grip on my arm. By then my cries were coming in short gasps, and it was with shaky hands that I reached to pull up my pants.

"Quit all that sniveling, boy!" she grumbled. I swallowed hard, trying to compose myself quickly. I didn't want to give her a reason to hit me anymore. Once I was dressed, I swiped at my tear-stained face. I looked down at the boards on the porch, afraid to look her in the eye. After a whipping we had to wait for her to tell us to go away before we could move. Sometimes the waiting was just as bad as the whipping itself.

"Don't ya defy me anymore, ya hear?"

"Yes, ma'am," I said softly, thankful that my voice had been clear. There was no way that I wanted to give her a reason to yell some more.

"Get out of here." I peeked up at her and watched as she disappeared into the house. I should have been relieved that it was all over, but instead I was confused. Was I supposed to go inside and clean up the footprints, or should I go back to the barn with Vic? I'd just assumed that she would tell me to come in and clean my mess, but since she hadn't, I didn't know what to do. I stood still on the porch trying to come up with the right answer. Mrs. Borg had said to stay out of the house, but at the same time, she was always after Vic and me to clean up behind us.

After a couple seconds of contemplation I decided that it would be best to clean up the footprints. I leaned against the hand pump and balanced on one foot to take off a shoe at a time. It was awkward trying to accomplish that, but sitting down was not an option. My butt was still stinging! I put my shoes on the steps and quietly entered the house with my holey, sock-covered feet. I'd only taken a few steps before stopping in my tracks. Mrs. Borg was on her hands and knees cleaning the footprints I'd made. Even though I'd been careful not to slam the screen, the soft thump of the door made her look up.

There were many times since I'd arrived there that I'd wished I were invisible. This was definitely another one of those times. One look at me and it was clear that her fiery anger was stoked again.

"I don't believe ya in here again!" she said incredulously, as she rose to her feet. She was in front of me after two quick steps. "I'll teach ya," she said, snatching me again by my already sore left arm.

She stormed out the door, dragging me along behind her. I had to almost run to keep from falling down, and I stumbled several times, trying to keep up with her quick pace. I think my heart was beating as fast as my legs were moving. I was nervous, wondering what she was going to do to me. We were heading toward the barn when suddenly she stopped in the middle of the yard near a large red brick. She abruptly let go of my arm, and my momentum made me fall to the ground. I scrambled to get up, but Mrs. Borg stopped me.

"Stay down there," she grumbled. "Get on your knees right there," she pointed to the brick that was in front of me. I looked up at her, confused.

What on earth was she talking about? Why did she want me to get on my knees on top of a brick?

"Ya still want to disobey me, huh?" Her voice was sharp as she gave me a shove in the direction of the brick. "Get down there."

I fell back down, surprised by her actions. My knee scraped across the rough surface of the brick, and I whimpered softly from the pain. When I was on both knees I looked up at her. She was glaring at me, a look that I was all too familiar with.

"Now, you stay right there till I say get up," she said harshly. Then, without waiting for me to answer, she turned on her heels and went back to the house. The screen door slammed closed behind her.

A few minutes passed.

I knelt there as I'd been told, patiently waiting for her to return. I realized that this was my punishment for coming into the house when I shouldn't have, although I figured I probably would have been punished even if I hadn't tried to come in and clean up behind myself.

Punishment for Vic and I was a way of life by now. I don't think either of us went more than two days without doing something that Mrs. Borg decided deserved a few licks from her switch.

More time passed, and I could feel beads of sweat forming across the top of my forehead. The sun was beating down unmercifully. I shifted a little, wondering when I would be allowed to get up. Not only were my knees beginning to feel sore, but my legs were falling asleep as well.

I stared at the kitchen window, trying to see if I'd catch a glimpse of Mrs. Borg watching me, but I saw no one. I rocked back on my heels, trying to take some of the weight off my knees. My knees were on fire.

"Straighten up!" Mrs. Borg yelled through the window. I looked up, and this time I saw her watching me through the curtains. I straightened my back, resting my full weight on my knees. Pain shot through my legs, and I cried out. Moments later I heard the crunch of gravel behind me. Vic had come running from around the side of the barn to see what was going on. When he saw me, he gave me a puzzled look.

"Ronnie, what are you doing?" he asked.

"Get away from there!" yelled Mrs. Borg. She had stepped back onto the porch and was waving her hands in our direction as if she was shooing flies.

"Why do ya have Ronnie sitting here?" he asked. "He didn't do anything. He was just trying to help me."

By that time Vic was standing right next to me. I felt a little better that he was there with me, but I had the feeling that he was going to end up getting in trouble himself.

"Get away from me," Mrs. Borg repeated. She had come down off the porch and was storming in our direction.

"Get out of here, Vic," I said through clenched teeth. There was no point in both of us getting punished over some toilet paper.

But Vic didn't move. He stood there defiantly and was met with a thundering backhand for his trouble. I shuddered as Vic stumbled backward from the intensity of the blow. She rarely hit us with her bare hands, so I was sure that the smack had stunned Vic just as much as it hurt him. But when my brother fell down and didn't get up, I got worried.

"Vic, get up," I called. I wanted to run to him, but Mrs. Borg was standing too close for me to even think of moving. She'd surely catch me before I could get to him. I guess she sensed my contemplation.

"Don't even think about moving, boy," she said, gruffly.

"Get up," she yelled in Vic's direction.

When my brother still didn't move, Mrs. Borg trudged over to him. She nudged him with a toe, but Vic lay motionless. Mrs. Borg squatted down beside my brother. Her eyes squinted as she looked down on him. She placed a hand on his forehead and frowned. Then she mumbled under her breath and scooped him up in her arms.

When she stood up, so did I. I intended to follow her into the house. Something was wrong with my brother, and I didn't want to let him out of my sight. I was certain that this woman had done something to him, and this scared me.

What would I do without Vic?

Mrs. Borg started toward the house, and I fell in step a few paces behind her. I managed to make it all the way to the porch before she realized that I was with her. She was struggling to open the screen door, so I jumped in front and pulled it open. I held it long enough for her to walk through, and I was about to come inside when she looked over her shoulder at me.

"Just where do you think you're going? It's because of your hardheaded behind that he's like this! Now get back out there like I told ya to! And this time don't move till I say so, if you know what's good for you!"

I stopped dead in my tracks. This was *my* fault? The weight of her words caused my whole body to shake with fear. Was I really responsible for Vic being like this? Of course I was, I concluded. If I hadn't cried out, Vic wouldn't have come running to check on me. And if he hadn't come running, Mrs. Borg wouldn't have smacked him so hard.

Yes, it was my fault.

I hung my head in shame and went back out to the brick. I knelt down and stared back at the house through misty eyes. Vic was my best friend, and now I'd done something to get him hurt. It was then that I knew I was truly a bad person. No wonder nobody wanted me.

By the time the doctor showed up about two hours later, I was drenched with sweat. I hadn't seen Mrs. Borg since she'd gone in with Vic. I caught a glimpse of her when she came to the screen to let the doctor in. I stared in her direction, trying to will her to look my way, hoping she'd let me up. But to my dismay, she ignored me, and the two of them disappeared inside. I swallowed, trying to get rid of the thick lump in my throat, but my mouth was so dry that it didn't do much good.

Several minutes later the doctor emerged from the house. When he stepped off the porch onto the gravel road, he looked over at me. I gave him a hopeful smile, thinking that maybe he would come tell me how Vic was doing. Instead he shook his head in what appeared to be displeasure. Obviously he knew that this whole thing was my fault too. That made him one more person who didn't like me. Fresh tears covered my face, and I wondered why on earth I'd ever been born.

The sun had long since set, and the night air had begun to chill my damp body when Mr. Borg came out of the house to call me in for supper. By that time my legs were completely numb, and when I tried to stand they tingled as if they were being pricked by hundreds of needles.

After several attempts I began to feel the circulation coming back to my stiff limbs and managed to get up. I moved slowly, feeling as though I would collapse at any moment. I hadn't eaten since breakfast, and that was hours ago. I stopped to wash my hands at the pump before going inside. There were only three place settings at the table. The missing one of course was Vic's. Seeing the empty space made my heart sink. Suddenly the ravenous hunger I'd felt dissipated. When Mrs. Borg set my plate in front of me, I barely looked at it.

Both the Borgs were eating heartily until they noticed that I hadn't as much as picked up my fork. Mr. Borg looked at me, then at Mrs. Borg.

"Your brother is okay, Ronnie. He just has the flu, that's all," said Mr. Borg softly.

Instantly I perked up. The flu was something that just happened. It wasn't anything that I'd caused, and it wasn't something that Mrs. Borg had made happen to him because of me. Knowing that made me feel better. It also explained why he'd been running to the bathroom so much. I picked up my fork and dug into my meatloaf and mashed potatoes.

Chapter Twelve:
Swinging from the Rafters

AFTER VIC'S BOUT WITH THE FLU, WE RECEIVED A VISIT FROM A social worker named Ms. Wilson. By that time we'd been living with the Borgs for over a year, and the social worker was there to see how we were doing.

She sat with us outside near the barn, presumably so that we could have some privacy. She was a tall, pleasant looking woman with an accent that we'd never heard before. When she asked us questions, it was sometimes hard to understand her, and she would have to repeat them. Thankfully she was patient and didn't yell at us. Not that I said anything anyway.

Even though I wanted to tell Ms. Wilson how much I hated being with the Borgs, I was too shy to do it. The fear of not knowing what she would do with the information we gave her was enough to keep me silent. Vic, on the other hand, spouted off about everything that had happened to us. He told her about the beatings, the nights with no supper, and the awful things Mrs. Borg said to us.

"She's always calling Ronnie stupid," Vic said emphatically.

"Is that true?" Ms. Wilson asked. The sudden shift of attention in my direction caught me off guard. Throughout Vic's whole tirade against the Borgs, Ms. Wilson had only nodded and scribbled things down in her notebook. Now she was looking at me, waiting for me to corroborate what Vic had said. And of course that was the very moment that my tongue refused to work correctly.

"Y-y-yes," I stammered.

Ms. Wilson stared at me for a moment, and then scribbled some more in her notebook. When she looked up at me again, she shook her head slightly and frowned. My face was hot. The expression on her face was clear to me. She thought I was stupid too.

After that she only talked to us for a few more minutes before going in to talk to Mr. and Mrs. Borg. Vic and I sat outside on the porch and waited. My stomach pitched with anxiety. I wondered how much Ms. Wilson would tell them about what Vic had said. Of course it really didn't matter. Any of it was enough to get us in trouble. I was thinking about what our punishment might be when something totally unexpected happened.

"Come on in here, boys."

The sound of Mrs. Borg's voice calling us into the house startled us both. We weren't usually allowed inside until suppertime, for one thing, and the tone of her voice was much too pleasant, for another. I looked at Vic quizzically, but he just shrugged his shoulders. He was as surprised as I was.

"Well, come on," Mrs. Borg called again. This time she was standing right in front of the screen door. In her hand was a large plate piled with cookies. Vic stood up slowly, looking puzzled. I didn't move though. I wasn't sure what to make of her sudden change of demeanor, but I didn't trust it.

"Ronnie, don't you want any of my cookies?" she asked sweetly.

My jaw dropped. She was offering us cookies? We were hardly ever given anything sweet. Mrs. Borg didn't normally bake unless it was a special occasion, and sometimes not even then. But now here she was offering us cookies.

Was this some sort of trick?

I sniffed the sweet smell of the freshly baked cookies. If it was a trick, I didn't care. I jumped up from the stairs and went inside with my brother. Ms. Wilson was sitting at the table talking with Mr. Borg when we walked in. When she heard the scuffing sound of out boots, she stopped mid-sentence and looked over at us.

"It seems that things are going just fine here," she said, closing her notebook. "You boys are very lucky to have the Borgs."

She shot a scolding look in each of our directions. It wasn't at all hard to figure out what it meant. Nothing we'd told her mattered. The Borgs had disposed of any accusations we may have made. Suddenly the cookie in my mouth tasted more like a dry piece of cardboard. No doubt about it, Vic and I were in for it as soon as Ms. Wilson left.

"Thank you both for being so hospitable," Ms. Wilson gushed, as she took another cookie. She stood to leave, and Mrs. Borg walked with her to the door.

As soon as the two women left the room, Mr. Borg got up and went to his bedroom to get ready for work.

"Now what?" I asked when Vic and I were alone at the table. "You know we're gonna get it."

At first Vic didn't answer. In fact, he didn't even look as if he'd heard me. Next thing I knew he jumped up from the table and dashed to the screen door. I watched him peek outside, then come streaking back into the dining room.

"Take some of those cookies and come on," he said, hurriedly.

"Huh?" What in the world was wrong with him? He had to know that those cookies weren't really meant for us.

"Grab some of those cookies," he hissed. "Hurry up!"

The urgency in his voice made me hop up from my seat and do what he said. He was grabbing handfuls of the cookies and stuffing them into a pouch that he'd made by lifting the tail end of his shirt. Although I didn't know how Vic figured we were going to get away with this, I followed suit.

"That's enough," he whispered. "Follow me."

Vic took off for the stairs, and it was then that I realized what his plan was. We were going to stash the cookies in our room. Vic took the stairs two at a time, with me right behind him. Once we were in our room, he stopped and scanned the room for a good hiding place.

"What about in there?" I asked, pointing my toe at the black duffel bag that was halfway under the bed.

"Yeah, that's good," he said. We dumped the cookies into the bag hurriedly, dropping several of them in the process. When we finished, we did our best to scatter the crumbs around so they couldn't be seen.

"We'd better get back downstairs," I said nervously. I could just imagine Mrs. Borg sneaking upstairs and catching us. The thought of the type of whipping that would bring made me shudder. We clumped quickly back down the stairs, our boots making far too much noise, but we didn't have time to be concerned about that. We were more interested in saving our butts.

Mrs. Borg's heavy footsteps, followed by the squeaking sound of the opening screen door, met us as we slid into our seats. Seconds later she appeared in the dining room. All traces of any smile on her face had been replaced with that scowl Vic and I had grown accustomed to. Things were back to normal now.

"What are you still sitting here for?" she snarled. "Don't you have chores to tend to?"

Neither of us said a word. It wasn't as if Mrs. Borg really wanted an answer from us. What she wanted was for us to get out of the house, which is what we got up to do. We were only a few steps from the safety of the outdoors when her voice thundered behind us.

"You gluttons ate all those cookies!"

We both froze momentarily and then bolted through the door. It was certain that Mrs. Borg would get us for taking the cookies and leaving while she was talking to us, but we'd deal with that later in the evening.

Once inside the barn we climbed up into the loft and flopped down on the scattered hay. My heart was still racing from running so fast, and I lay there breathing heavily. When Vic started laughing, I sat up and looked at him.

"Can you imagine what her face looked like when she saw all those cookies gone?" he asked in between chuckles.

I thought about it for a moment and then burst into a fit of laughter as well. Mrs. Borg was probably fuming! It had no doubt been extremely hard for her to pretend to be nice to us for the duration of Ms. Wilson's visit, especially since she didn't have much practice in doing so. I was willing to bet that even Mr. Borg was surprised by her act, although he didn't show it.

Mr. Borg didn't show emotion about too much of anything. We barely saw him. He was either at work or sleeping to get ready to go to work. The other times, he was in the field until suppertime. And then when we saw him at suppertime, he didn't really say much. I wondered what he thought about how Mrs. Borg treated us.

Soon after the social worker's visit, when we were at school and the neighbor came to pick us up, which never happened before, she informed us that Mr. Borg had been in a major tractor accident while working in the field. We were sent to Mr. Borg's sister's house in Aurora, Illinois. We were told that Mr. Borg had lost his leg in the accident. It was at least a month or more before we were back on the farm.

We thought things were bad before, but they were about to get twice as bad. When we saw Mr. Borg for the first time he was no longer a large, strong man but a man with one leg getting around in a wheelchair, and because of the pain medicine, he had become withdrawn and a meek man. Mrs. Borg had become even angrier, if possible, and would take her anger out on Vic and me. What we didn't understand was why the state didn't take us away because of what happened.

"Hey, Vic, do you think Mr. Borg ever says anything to her about how mean she is?" Even though I doubted that he did, I wanted to know what my brother thought.

"Nawww," he said, after a second of contemplation.

"He probably doesn't get a chance to say much. He probably doesn't care about us anyhow. Why should he?"

Vic got up. "Forget them." He walked over and grabbed onto a rope that was hanging from the rafters. "Betcha I can make across to the other side," he said.

"No you can't," I said with a smile. We'd been trying to reach the other loft by swinging across that rope for months. So far neither of us had succeeded in making it, but of the two of us, I'd come the closest.

"Yeah, I can," he said. He pushed off from the edge of the platform and swung through the air. I held my breath as I watched him hurtle toward the other side. But he didn't have enough momentum, and the rope stopped way short of the next platform. His body began to swing back to where I was standing.

"Ha!" I exclaimed tauntingly. "You didn't even get close!"

Vic landed back on the platform and passed me the rope. "Here, you still can't do it either," he challenged.

With a cocky smile, I grabbed the rope and carefully positioned it between my legs. I took a few extra steps backward for a running start, and then sailed off the platform. I was going to do it this time—I could feel it.

The rafter groaned from the pull of the rope as it propelled me through the air. The edge of the platform was almost within my reach, so I unwrapped my legs from around the rope. My success wouldn't count if I made it to the other side but didn't manage to get off the rope. Because I'd never gotten quite this close before, I'd never unwrapped my legs before, and because of that I had no idea how much my legs were a part of what kept me up on that rope. My dangling legs felt heavy, and my hands began to slip.

Panic ran through me, and I flailed my legs wildly, trying to get my footing onto the platform, but the idea backfired. All the wiggling of my body disrupted the natural swinging of the rope, and instead of continuing toward the other side, the rope began to swing from side to side, and my momentum slowed down.

I pumped my legs trying to keep from stopping but the rope continued to slow down. By then, I was swinging back and forth like a pendulum. Not slow enough to jump off, but not fast enough to reach either side of the loft.

"Help me, Vic!" I yelled. When I looked down, the ground seemed extremely far away. I had no idea how I was going to get off the rope, but by then, I desperately wanted off.

"Hang on, Ronnie," he called, as he scrambled down the ladder. In a flash he was standing below me on the barn floor, trying to grab the end of the rope.

Unfortunately he was too short and couldn't reach it. Fear gripped me, and my hands started to perspire. I slipped a few more inches.

"Hurry, Vic!" My voice wavered, and I was on the verge of tears. If he didn't figure out how to get me down soon, I was going to fall.

Just as I thought that, my hands slid even further, and for the first time, I felt the slicing burn of the rope go through my hands. There were only a few feet of rope left for me to hold on to.

"Pull yourself up, Ronnie," Vic said.

On the ground, he still obviously had not figured out how to get me down, because he was pacing back and forth beneath me. I struggled with the rope, while trying to inch my legs upward. But as soon as I let go with one hand, the other hand slid down the rope, and I plummeted to the ground.

When I finally opened my eyes, Mrs. Borg was standing over me, muttering under her breath. I blinked and then squeezed my eyes shut. My head ached terribly, and my face felt hot. I wanted to get up, but it was too difficult. My body wouldn't cooperate. I closed my eyes again, and everything faded to black.

Vic was grinning down at me when I woke up again. This time I was lying in my bed. My head was still throbbing, but not as bad as it had been earlier.

"You got a big knot on your head," Vic said, still smiling.

Immediately I reached for the back of my head. There was indeed a large lump on the back of my head. I winced when my hand touched it. It hurt something awful.

I wiggled the rest of my body. Arms, legs, hands, everything else seemed to be okay. Luckily I'd fallen on a bed of hay. But why did my head hurt so much?

"The doctor was here," Vic volunteered. "He said you got a concussion." Vic seemed proud of my battle scar, which meant that Mrs. Borg was probably furious.

I struggled to get up, but a sharp wave of pain shot through my head, and I collapsed back down on my pillow.

"Ouch!" I squeezed my eyes shut to keep from crying.

"You gotta lay down for a couple of days," Vic said solemnly. "The doctor said."

A couple of days seemed like a long time. I couldn't imagine having to stay in the house that long, nor could I believe that Mrs. Borg was at all pleased about it. Besides, with me in bed, that would mean that Vic had to do all the chores by himself. It was hard enough for us to finish them together. Doing them alone would be almost impossible.

"But I gotta help you," I protested half-heartedly. The throbbing in my head was returning, and with each movement it began to get worse.

"It's okay," he said. "I can do it by myself."

The sounds of footsteps coming up the stairs quieted us both. They weren't heavy, so we knew it wasn't Mrs. Borg. Our eyes were glued to the door as we waited to see who was coming. It was Mr. Borg.

"Vic," he said quietly, "come on so we can get these chores out of the way." He looked at me briefly. "How're you feeling, Ronnie?"

"My head hurts," I answered.

"I'll bet it does," he said, smiling a little. "That was quite a fall you had. You boys have got to be more careful. I can't take off from work anymore for things like this."

His tone changed a little when he said that. It wasn't quite as friendly as it had been, but it wasn't angry either. It was hard to tell if he was upset, especially since he hardly ever spoke to us.

"Let's go, Vic." The two of them turned and walked away. Vic looked back at me over his shoulder and smiled.

Chapter Thirteen:
Running Away

BEFORE WE KNEW IT, WE HAD BEEN WITH THE BORGS FOR FIVE years. Both Vic and I were in school, and although it provided an escape from Mrs. Borg's constant nagging, it wasn't a pleasant experience either.

Almost from day one, the kids teased me about one thing or another. My clothes, the way we smelled, my speech, it was always something. It got to the point where I couldn't stand to be at school.

The day came when I'd finally had enough. It had been a typical morning. Vic and I arose early to do some of our chores before going to school. We fed the chickens, collected eggs, and slopped the pigs as usual, and left the other tasks for when we returned. We were getting ready to get on the road to walk to school when Mrs. Borg stopped us.

"I'm going in to town, so you two can hop on the tractor with me."

I groaned inwardly. Even though the walk to school was a long one, it still beat riding on the back of that dirty tractor.

I hated it because it got our clothes so dusty, and it always seemed to leave us smelling like the animals. And, of course, that was one of the main reasons that we were always being teased.

"We can walk, ma'am," I said, looking at Vic to back me up. I knew that speaking up was likely to spark her anger, but it didn't matter. There were times when her yelling didn't seem to compare to the cruelty of the kids at school.

"I don't need ya to tell me what ya can do," she said stonily. "I told the two of ya to come on with me!"

I thought for a moment, wondering if it would be worth it to anger her further and risk a spanking. Just when I was coming to understanding her.

"C'mon, Ronnie," he said.

I pulled my arm away. Vic looked at me strangely, then turned away and followed behind Mrs. Borg. I stood there, upset with Vic for not taking my side. Even though he didn't have quite as hard a time fitting in at school as I did, I thought he would at least stick with me. I sighed and walked slowly to the tractor.

When we arrived in front of the school, there were a bunch of kids playing together waiting for the bell to ring. The loud rattling sound of the tractor made them stop what they were doing and look in our direction. As soon as Vic and I climbed down, the kids began snickering and pointing. I hung my head and headed straight for the classroom. Any chance I'd had of getting in on a game of tag had been ruined by a tractor ride.

Soon after we arrived the bell rang, and the rest of the kids in my class trooped in. A few of them continued to giggle as they passed me while others made sniffing sounds. I sunk further down into my seat. Every day I wished I could become invisible, but I hadn't been able to do it so far. So until I was able to completely disappear, sinking down into my seat as far as I could was the best I could do.

On most days, our lessons started with math, but on this particular morning our teacher, Mrs. King, decided to change the schedule. She told us to pull out our reading books and then began choosing students to read aloud. I was chosen to read second. As if my day wasn't already going bad enough.

My heart was pounding so hard that I thought I could feel it coming out of my chest. I waited my turn, praying that some miracle would happen that would keep me from stuttering. But of course I knew that miracles didn't happen, at least not for me, so I prayed for a distraction that would keep me from having to take my turn. Neither of those things happened, and once my classmate, Margaret, finished reading, Mrs. King moved in front of me.

"Ronnie, please read the next three paragraphs."

I took a deep breath and stared down at the page. The words glared out at me, and my heartbeat thundered in my ears. I tried to swallow, but my mouth was so dry, it didn't do much good. After another deep breath, I opened my mouth and started reading the words on the page.

At first my words came out clearly, which was a shock to me, but by the middle of the first paragraph I began to stumble, and my face became flush.

"Told you he was a dummy," whispered one of the boys a few seats over.

"Why does he even come to school?" someone else asked.

Tears welled up in my eyes against my will. I stopped trying to read and swiped away at them quickly. I was called so many different names, I didn't want them to add crybaby to the list. Snickers sputtered through the room, and Mrs. King quickly hushed them. She gave me a sympathetic look and moved to the next student.

By lunchtime I'd had enough of school and the Borgs. Since none of the kids paid any attention to me anyway, it was easy to slip behind a tree and out of the schoolyard without being seen. I trudged down the dusty trail toward town. I had no idea where I was going, but it didn't matter. As far as I was concerned, anywhere was better than where I'd been. After about thirty minutes of walking, I started to feel bad about leaving Vic behind. The feeling quickly subsided when I thought of how he'd treated me earlier that morning. If only he'd decided to walk with me, maybe the day wouldn't have been quite as bad.

When I reached town, I didn't know what to do. The sun was beating down on me and my throat was parched. By that time I knew that school was over and that Vic was probably wondering where I was. I figured he'd look for me for a while before leaving. I thought about what Mrs. Borg would say once he got home without me. Most likely she'd scream at him, but I hoped that she wouldn't spank him because of me.

I walked around town, avoiding the looks of grown-ups. Occasionally I stopped and peered inside the large store windows. It was getting later and later, and pretty soon my stomach rumbled hungrily. The sun was sinking, and I imagined that Vic was just about finished with the chores. It was almost suppertime, and I had no idea as to what I would eat. For that matter I didn't even know where I would sleep.

Several hours had passed since I left school and I was very tired and very hungry. The town was fairly small, and I had walked around the same area more times than I could count. I was approaching the grocery store again and decided to sit down and rest. There was a stoop near the entrance, and I plopped down on it wearily. Men and women looked at me curiously as they entered and exited the store. I didn't recognize any of them, and that disappointed me. Perhaps if I could find someone who knew the Borgs, they would feel sorry enough for me that they would take me home with them.

Another hour passed. The wind was biting, and I was close to tears. An elderly woman came out of the store and stood in front of me.

"Are your parents in the store?" she asked.

I shook my head sadly. "No, ma'am."

"Well, where are they?" she asked, curiously.

"At home," I said, quietly.

"Well then, you should go home," she said sternly.

Her tone was crisp and almost as icy as the wind that had started to pick up as night fell. My tears were hot, but quickly cooled on my cheeks when the air hit them. I shivered.

As much as I didn't want to agree, the old woman was right. I had nowhere to go, and during times like these, it was ridiculous for me to think that someone else would take me home with them. The reality was that I had no choice but to go back to the Borgs. I stood up, stepped down off the stoop, and began the long walk home. By the time I got back to the farm it was very late. For some reason it surprised me that neither Mr. nor Mrs. Borg was on the road looking for me.

Instead, the house was dark. I walked onto the porch and pulled on the screen door, praying that it wouldn't squeak. Even though I knew I wouldn't avoid punishment, I hoped to at least delay it until morning. At that moment I was exhausted, and I only wanted to sleep.

Despite my caution, the door squeaked noisily. I winced, then waited. I expected Mrs. Borg to come fling the door open, breathing fire, at any moment. When nothing happened after a few seconds, I reached for the doorknob. It wouldn't turn. The door was locked.

My heart sank. I slid down to the floor and burst into tears. I was cold, tired, and hungry, and now I was locked out of the house. I got up slowly and tried to close the screen quietly. Just as I was about to walk off the porch the front door creaked open. I stopped, sure that I was dead.

"Ronnie!" At the sound of Vic's whisper, I spun around. I couldn't remember a time that I was happier to see him.

"C'mon," he whispered urgently. I smiled weakly and hurried through the screen door. The two of us moved quickly and quietly up the stairs, avoiding the creaky boards. When we got into our room, Vic looked at me angrily. "Where'd you go?"

I shook my head sadly. I didn't want to talk about where I'd been. At least not right then. Since I couldn't eat, I simply wanted to sleep. I peeled off my clothes and hopped into bed. Vic was still standing in the middle of the floor, staring at me.

"Please don't be mad, Vic," I said desperately.

He frowned for a second, then grinned at me.

"Hungry?" he asked.

I bobbed my head up and down vigorously. I should have known that I could count on Vic to save me something.

I watched as he went to one of the dresser drawers. He reached under the clothes and came out with something wrapped in a towel. My stomach growled violently as the smell of what was inside began to permeate through the layers of the towel.

Finally he unveiled a thick pork chop. I looked at him in disbelief. I couldn't imagine how he'd managed to sneak something so big off the table.

Over the years we had gotten good at saving food from dinner and sneaking it to our rooms for later. But it had always been small things, like biscuits or an occasional chicken leg. However he'd been able to do it didn't matter though. I thankfully accepted the food from my brother and took a huge bite.

"What was it like?" Vic asked curiously. I chewed thoughtfully.

"It was terrible," I said finally. "There was nothing to do but wander around. People looked at me funny."

"I didn't think you were coming back," he said, sounding worried. "Mrs. Borg was really mad!" Vic chuckled. "She was screaming about how ungrateful we were, and that she didn't care if you came back or not."

My eyes widened. If Mrs. Borg had felt that way, I wondered how she would react when she saw me in the morning. That was of course after she spanked me first.

Maybe she will call the agency and they'll take me away.

The idea of that didn't seem so bad, but then I began to think.

What if they send me away without Vic?

That saddened me. Just because I'd left school by myself, didn't mean I wanted to be somewhere else without Vic. I finished my pork chop and settled down to go to sleep. My punishment would come at the crack of dawn. I just hoped that it didn't include being away from my brother.

I received my usual punishment, but I was still with my brother, and for that I was happy.

Despite my desire to stay with my brother my unhappiness at the Borgs' caused me to hit the road several more times over the next two years. It usually happened after a disheartening visit by one of the social workers. Vic and I would complain about the way we were treated, and the social workers would ignore us. They were always reminding us that we were lucky to have found a home and that there were dozens of children who hadn't been so fortunate.

After each visit things got worse for about a week. It seemed that Mrs. Borg became angry with us for just being around. Everything we did was wrong, and the beatings came more frequently. Several times I took some clothes and food we stashed from dinner and disappeared into the night. As usual, I didn't have much of a plan, so I ended up returning to face the music. It was a cycle that went on and on, seemingly without end. We were stuck with the Borgs, and there wasn't a thing we could do about it.

Chapter Fourteen:
The Accident

I HAD JUST ABOUT GIVEN UP PRAYING FOR THINGS TO CHANGE when very abruptly they did. Vic was thirteen and I was twelve. Eight years had passed since we arrived at the Borgs, and surprisingly we had found a way to survive. It was a Saturday afternoon, and Vic and I were dragging freshly bundled bales of hay into the barn. Mr. Borg was driving the tractor in the field and the horrible Mrs., which was what we now called Mrs. Borg, was somewhere in the house. The heat was bearing down on us, and as soon as we finished with the last bale, Vic and I collapsed on the barn floor.

"You wanna play horseshoes later?" I asked Vic, as I stared up into the rafters. We usually played once we finished our chores. I'd gotten good over the last year, and it had become much harder for Vic to beat me.

"Yeah, sure," he said, chewing on a piece of hay. I looked over at my brother. There was a scowl on his face as if he were deep in thought. I was just about to ask him what was on his mind when a loud scream rang out. The two of us scrambled toward the sound of the anguished cries. It was coming from out in the field. We ran swiftly in that direction, nearly colliding with Mrs. Borg, who had come running from inside the house.

As we got closer, we could hear the tractor motor. It was making a grinding sound that sputtered at intervals and mixed horribly with Mr. Borg's screams. We all reached him at the same time, and the sight staggered me. Blood was everywhere. Mr. Borg lay on the ground, his leg a tattered mess beneath the teeth of the huge tractor. The teeth spun and then halted, which explained the grinding sound we'd heard. I watched, paralyzed to my spot. Vic passed by me and hopped onto the tractor. He killed the engine as Mrs. Borg raced over to her husband.

"Go to the neighbors quick," she cried over her shoulder. I didn't move. I couldn't. I'd never seen so much human blood in my life. And to see Mr. Borg on the ground writhing in pain scared me.

"Go, Ronnie," said Vic. He nudged me in the direction of the road, then rushed over to help Mrs. Borg.

After one more glance at them, I took off like a shot. I sprinted down the driveway and onto the dirt road. The closest neighbor was a little over a mile away, but I made it in record time. When I got there, I banged loudly on the door. A few minutes later Mr. Peters came from around the side of the house.

"What on earth are you doing, boy?" he asked, his voice filled with annoyance.

"Come quick," I said breathlessly. "Mr. Borg's been hurt."

"What?" Mr. Peters threw down his rake and hurried over to me.

"The tractor," I gulped air. "His leg …"

"C'mon, boy," he said, grabbing me by the arm.

We spent weeks at the Peters' house while Mr. Borg was in the hospital. Before and after school we were required to go to the farm and do our regular chores, as well as any chores that Mr. Peters had for us. Needless to say we were exhausted every night, but it was an improvement from being at the Borgs. I secretly wished we didn't have to go back.

Though the Peters weren't overly nice, they were much more pleasant to be around, and they didn't yell the way Mrs. Borg did. In fact, Mr. Peters sometimes played horseshoes with us. It was a strange yet nice change to hear the voice of a man around the house. While Mr. Borg rarely spoke, Mr. Peters talked incessantly. He was a know-it-all who always inserted his opinion about everything.

Regretfully, the day for our return to the Borgs house came. It was late in the evening when Mr. Peters drove us there. He parked in front of the house, and we all just sat there for a few minutes. None of us were sure what to expect. Mrs. Peters had told us a few days ago that the tractor had done so much damage to Mr. Borg's leg that the doctor had to amputate it. I'd spent most of the night before trying to imagine what that would look like. I'd never known a person could manage with one leg, let alone seen anyone like that.

"Let's go," said Mr. Peters.

Mrs. Borg must have heard the slamming of the truck doors, because she was at the front door before we stepped onto the porch. We hadn't seen her the entire time that we'd been gone, and somehow she looked different. Her face was drawn, and she was a little thinner. The only thing that hadn't changed was her mean expression and her ugly disposition.

We were barely inside before she began growling a bunch of do's and don'ts at us.

"Keep quiet, and don't go asking a bunch of questions! And don't stare at him!"

Neither of us said a word, only nodded our heads. Since she'd already told us to keep quiet we saw no need to verbalize our understanding of her instructions. We were certain that the less talking we did, the better. She looked us over, contemplating whether she needed to bark at us anymore. Once she was sure we understood her, she smiled at Mr. Peters and led us into their bedroom.

Mr. Borg had never been a very large man. In fact, compared to his wife, he was somewhat dwarfed. From first glance, it was obvious that during his stay at the hospital, Mr. Borg had also lost weight. He was pale and looked as though he had aged tremendously in the weeks since we'd seen him last.

Mr. Peters walked right up alongside the bed and sat in a chair that was there. Vic and I hung back by the door and watched as the two men talked. Thankfully, Mrs. Borg had gone to the kitchen right after she'd ushered us to the bedroom. With her out of the way, we were able to study Mr. Borg without fear of reprimand. But there wasn't really much to see. His body was concealed under the covers, so we couldn't see the space where his leg used to be. I wasn't quite sure I wanted to see it anyway.

"Boys, come on in," Mr. Borg beckoned us over.

We both hung back at first, waiting for the other to take the first step. But after seeing that I wasn't going to budge, Vic walked slowly over to the bed. I followed reluctantly.

"Mr. Peters tells me the two of you were a big help to him on his farm," he said. "I'm glad you earned your keep. Gonna be a lot of things need doing back here. Mr. Peters is gonna come over and help with some of the fieldwork. That means no goofing off in the barn." He looked directly at me when he said it.

"Yes, sir," we said in unison.

"Good, now you two go on out of here while I finish talking to Mr. Peters."

I hurried out of the room first. His dismissal was not a moment too soon. I had begun to feel uncomfortable when I saw Mr. Borg's good leg shifting under the cover while he spoke. It was then that I noticed the differences in the length of each leg. I shuddered to think of what it actually looked like underneath. I was in such a rush to get out of there that I nearly knocked Mrs. Borg over.

"Watch it, boy," she grumbled.

"Sorry," I muttered, dodging out of her way. I took the stairs two at a time and retreated to my room. I flopped down on the bed. Vic came in a few minutes later.

"Pretty weird, huh?"

"Yeah," I answered quietly. "He's not ever gonna be able to do anything on the farm again."

Vic sighed. "Yeah, and we both know what that means."

I didn't say anything but I didn't have to. The weight of running the farm was going to fall on our shoulders, and like most everything else in our lives, we had no control over it.

Chapter Fifteen: The Final Straw

IN THE MONTHS THAT FOLLOWED VIC AND I ALL BUT GAVE UP GOING to school. Our chores had almost tripled. Just like Mr. Borg had said, Mr. Peters came over to help us with plowing the field, but that had been short lived. After two trips he quickly decided that the added work was more than he was willing to take on.

"Sorry, boys," he said one afternoon. "I've got my own farm to tend to, and it takes 'bout a full day just to plow yours. You two are gonna have to do it yourselves."

And just like that, he stopped coming over. He didn't bother to show us how to do the plowing or anything. Naturally, Mrs. Borg assumed that his absence had to do with something we'd done wrong. She ignored us when we tried to tell her what he'd said.

"Hush your mouths," she hissed. "You lazy, no account, good-for-nothings done run off the only help we had. Look at my field!"

In the two short weeks that Mr. Peters had stopped coming by, the field had grown almost as tall as we were. I could understand why Mrs. Borg was upset, at least about the way the field looked, but it still bothered me that she never believed anything we told her.

"Get out there and cut that field."

"But—" sputtered Vic.

"Don't give me any lip," she said, cutting him off. So we trudged off to try and make heads or tails of the task that lay before us. It took us the entire day to finish, and when we were done, we were exhausted but somewhat proud of ourselves. Although it didn't look like one of the men had done it, we hadn't completely butchered it either. Needless to say, Mrs. Borg pointed out all that was wrong with it that first time, but after a few weeks we mastered it, and her complaints stopped.

"I said I want another drink!"

The shouting and the crash of glass against the wall woke Vic and me instantly. Each of us sat straight up in bed and rubbed our eyes. We sat there listening as the yelling below us continued. Mr. Borg was drunk again. That was obvious by the slurring of his words when he spoke.

"And I said that you don't need another drink," Mrs. Borg screamed.

"Awww man," Vic groaned. "They're gonna keep us up again!"

He flopped back down on his pillow and covered his ears. I sighed loudly and lay back down too. For the last few months the fighting between the Borgs had become a nightly occurrence. Mr. Borg usually got up in the morning and hopped around on his crutches, getting in Mrs. Borg's way. After breakfast he would begin drinking, and pretty much throughout the day.

Since his accident he had transformed into an evil, bitter man who yelled obscenities at anybody who looked at him for too long. He was nothing like the quiet man that we'd met when we first came to the Borgs'. As if one screaming adult hadn't been enough, now Vic and I had to deal with two.

"Woman, if I say get me a drink, I mean it!"

"Shut up you old, one-legged drunk!"

Vic sat up again, his jaw dropped with surprise. I raised my eyebrows. In all the arguments we'd overheard, Mrs. Borg had never mentioned Mr. Borg having one leg. In fact, she had whipped Vic terribly for making the mistake of asking Mr. Borg how it felt to only have one leg.

All of a sudden everything was quiet. Vic and I strained to hear what was going on. It was hard to believe that Mr. Borg had not exploded over his wife's comments. Just when I was beginning to think that it was safe to go back to sleep, we heard the unmistakable click of Mr. Borg's shotgun.

"One-legged drunk," shouted Mr. Borg. "Woman, I'll kill you!"

The two of us shot up like rockets. We flew down the stairs and saw Mr. Borg standing near the sofa leaning on his crutch. He had his rifle in hand aimed directly at a very scared Mrs. Borg. She stood motionless near the old radio. Her face was pale, her eyes full of fear. When she heard us come downstairs she skirted a look in our direction but didn't say anything. I think that was the first time I'd ever seen her speechless.

Mr. Borg didn't pay any attention to us. His anger was trained on his wife, and that worked to our advantage. Both Vic and I bolted off the stairs and through the screen door into the night air. We'd moved so fast that I'm sure we must have looked like a blur to both the Borgs. Our feet barely hit the dirt road as we continued to run down the driveway in the direction of the Peters' house. By the time we reached their house, we were breathless. Vic and I pounded our fists against the front door.

"What on earth is wrong with you boys?" Mrs. Peters asked as she pulled her robe tight around her. Mr. Peters appeared behind her, holding his shotgun. When he saw that it was only us, he leaned it up against the door frame and looked at us curiously.

"What's going on, boys? What are you doing out here this time of night?"

"It's Mr. Borg," Vic began.

"He says he's gonna kill the Mrs.," I finished.

"Oh my Lord!" Mrs. Peters exclaimed. She turned to her husband. "You'd better get over there."

Mr. Peters grabbed his coat from the rack near the door and hurried onto the porch. He was halfway down the steps when he stopped and turned back. He reached inside the door, passed his wife, and snatched up his shotgun. Mrs. Peters gave him an alarmed look.

"If he's liquored up, I might need this," he said somberly. "No telling what that crazy fool might do."

Vic and I looked at each other. As unpredictable as Mr. Borg had been lately, the possibility of him actually shooting someone suddenly became very real. We rushed to the passenger side of Mr. Peters' truck and slid onto the cool vinyl seat. He turned the ignition, and the truck coughed loudly in the chilly night air. After a few sputtering attempts, the engine roared to life. Mr. Peters popped the gear in drive, and we sped down the road, leaving a cloud of dust behind us.

It surprised me to find the Borgs standing in the same spots that we'd left them in. I guessed we'd been gone at least fifteen minutes, yet Mrs. Borg was still glued to her spot near the radio. Her husband was still aiming his rifle at her.

Mr. Peters marched noisily onto the porch, but Vic and I hung back. We had no intention of returning inside that house until all guns were put away. In his current state, there was no telling what Mr. Borg might do, and we couldn't be sure that his anger wouldn't be sparked by Mr. Peters' arrival.

"Art, put that thing away," said Mr. Peters harshly.

At first I was a little confused. Who in the world was Art? And then I realized that Mr. Peters was talking to Mr. Borg. It may sound ridiculous, but in all our years with the Borgs, we'd never heard anyone call them by their first names.

"Told that woman to fix me a drink," Mr. Borg said stubbornly. "She keeps sassing me, calling me a drunk. I ought to kill her, bet that'd shut her up, eh?"

He chuckled, as if amused by the thought of shutting his wife up. I covered my face with my hands. If he was going to do it, I definitely didn't want to see it.

"No, Art," said Mr. Peters patiently. "You ought not kill her. That's your wife, and killing's bad anyhow. Now lemme hold that rifle."

He held his hand out. Mr. Borg eyed him suspiciously. "How come you want my rifle and you holding one in your hand?"

I held my breath. I wanted this entire scene to be over without incident, but Mr. Borg didn't seem willing to cooperate. Chills ran through me, and I couldn't help feeling fearful that Mr. Borg would indeed shoot someone. But then he seemed to have a change of heart. Surprisingly, he lowered his rifle and passed it to Mr. Peters. He looked at him, then at his wife.

"She isn't worth it nohow. I'll get my own drink."

He pulled his other crutch under his arm and took a step forward. His body swayed a little, and he took another step. The third step sent him crashing to the floor. The two grown-ups rushed over to him to help him up, but he was already passed out.

Another social worker showed up the very next morning. I doubt that it was by coincidence. More than likely, Mrs. Peters had contacted the agency after the previous night's events. Vic and I had opted to sleep out in the barn, even though Mr. Borg was out cold. We knew it wasn't likely that he'd wake up again before the morning, but it was sure better to be safe than sorry.

Since the visit was a surprise, Mrs. Borg had no way of denying the reports that the social worker had received. There was still broken glass on the floor in the living room, and the house was in general disarray. Aside from that, Mr. Borg was still feeling mean-spirited and definitely not on his best behavior.

The social worker didn't even bother to ask us how things were going. Instead she told us to go upstairs and pack all our belongings. Three jaws dropped open, mine, Vic's and Mrs. Borg's. When her words actually registered, Vic and I took off up the stairs. Clothes were shoved haphazardly into the black bag that we'd arrived with, and everything that didn't fit we piled into our arms. We wasted no time and were clumping back down the stairs in a flash. We didn't want Mrs. Borg to have the opportunity to change the social worker's mind about taking us away. And that is exactly what she was trying to do when we made it back to the living room.

"But who will help with the field?" she whined. I stopped in my tracks.

Please don't let her change her mind, I prayed.

My heart was in my throat while I waited for the woman to answer.

"That's not my problem," the social worker said with a shrug.

"Come on, boys. I have just the place for you."

It wasn't until the blue Chrysler began to roll down the driveway that I really believed we were leaving the Borgs'. After years of wishing, hoping, and praying, it had finally come true. I turned in my seat and watched from the rear window as the farm, the animals, and Mrs. Borg's permanent scowl, faded into a cloud of dust.

Red Cross Entry, dated November 7, 1958:

This needful boy is quick to say he is not wanted and has stated so regarding his foster home and school settings. Without doubt according to his interpretations there is merit to what Ronald says objectively, as well as according to his interpretations. Constant giving above the normal exchange expected may become tiresome or exhausting to school staff and peer groups. A slight cession of the amount previously extended may be easily interpreted by Ronald as being rejection as well as not being wanted.

Ronald does not like his foster mother and wants to be replaced even "if I have to go to an orphanage." His main reasons are that his foster mother doesn't want him, is always yelling at him, and is too bossy. Other reasons are that he is tired of being isolated on a farm as he can't go anywhere or do anything or make friends easily. Realistically, the farm is in semi isolation regarding proximity to the nearby community as well as it being true that use of the family car is limited since Mr. Borg drives it to work between 1 and 2:00 PM every day, except on weekends. Otherwise, Ronald is saying that his total needs have not been met which is true.

He is very likeable and relates quickly to those he feels are interested in him. Ronald is very sensitive and responds rapidly to positive and negative feelings transferred to him. His reaction to positive feelings is shown in a display of elative smiling, where his reaction to negative transfer feelings is exhibited by rejection, anger and disallusionment. Ronald is an appealing 12-year-old boy with dark brown hair, brown eyes, and a medium size build.

Most of his relationships are superficial, and some are manipulative. He will buy love, affection, and attention through manipulation if his physical appeal does not elicit his needs to be gratified.

Ronald is more prone to withholding his embittered feelings and sulking, as well as feeling self-pity rather than expression and the release of what is bothering him. He would give out dollar bills at school in his endeavor to purchase friendship.

Chapter Sixteen: The Hubers

"FIRST ONE FINISHES THREE LAPS GETS TO HAVE THE LOSER MAKE his bed for a whole week."

Charles was always making bets, but this was one I was certain he would lose. I'd become quite the swimmer in the four years that I'd been at ISSC, and very few boys had the nerve to challenge me in that area. But Charles was new, so he didn't know better yet. I fully intended to teach him. It would be nice to not have to worry about making my bed for a week.

ISSCS, the Illinois Soldiers and Sailors Children's Home, had been home to Vic and me since we left the Borgs' farm. It was a large area of land that consisted of several white cottages, a school, gymnasium, recreation room, and the indoor pool that I was now swimming in.

When we'd first arrived I'd been pretty skeptical. There were so many kids there that it reminded me of Covenant, but by that time, I'd given up hope of being sent somewhere halfway decent. I figured that this was the place they sent all the bad kids that no one wanted. In reality, it was nothing of the sort. ISSC was an orphanage, but the people that worked there were very nice.

**Fig. 16.1. An aerial view of
"The Illinois Soldiers and Sailors Children's Home."**

Our social worker introduced us to Mr. Jefferson, the gentleman who ran the entire school. He was a tall, beefy man with a deep, commanding voice that was very intimidating. At first I had little doubt he would be very hard on us, but that was not the case. Mr. Jefferson turned out to be an understanding man who wanted all the children at ISSC to have a good life.

Vic and I were separated shortly after we arrived. As it turned out, the cottages that we lived in grouped the boys together by certain ages. Since Vic was already a teenager he was sent to a different cottage than mine. I protested loudly when I learned we would not be together. As far as I was concerned, my brother was my one and only ally. My previous school had proven that I didn't make friends well, and I didn't relish the idea of being alone with a group of strangers who would probably make fun of me. But that was yet another decision that I had no control over.

For the most part I kept to myself those first few days. Without Vic to talk to, I felt extremely lost. As far as I could tell, the other boys had been there for quite some time. They were all very familiar with each other, and I didn't think there was any way that I'd fit in with them.

A week after our arrival, a boy named Joshua approached me and asked if I wanted to go with them to the recreation center. I'd been inclined to say no, but by then I was so lonely, I decided to take him up on his offer.

Before I knew it, I was friendly with most of the thirteen boys that shared the cottage with me. By friendly I mean that I was at least invited to play the games they played and they didn't treat me like a complete outcast. I still wasn't much of a talker. My stutter had been in hiding, but it wasn't completely gone. I worried constantly that if I got too nervous while I was talking, it would act up. I didn't want any of the other boys to hear it, didn't want to give them a reason to tease me.

I saw Vic during meals and when we spent time in the recreation room. He seemed to have made a lot of friends. And though he didn't ignore me, I didn't feel as close to him as I once had.

School was still one of my least favorite places. My teachers often commented that I needed to participate more. Participation meant raising my hand and asking questions, and that was something I didn't like to do. It drew too much attention to me, and I preferred to be left in obscurity.

One teacher in particular constantly questioned why I was such a withdrawn child. My answer to that was a shrug of my shoulders and a blank stare. How could I possibly explain to her that most of my life had been spent being invisible? I didn't trust the spotlight.

Overall life for my brother and I had been significantly better since we'd arrived at the Illinois Soldiers and Sailors Children's Home, in Normal, Illinois. The adults that worked there were nice to us. Even though we had homework and chores to do every day, we weren't treated like workhorses and were allowed to have fun. It had turned out to be the best place for Vic and me so far.

Things changed even more for me late during my junior year.

Most of the time I continued to be a loner, although I developed a friendship with a boy named Lonnie. Lonnie was in a couple of my classes and quite a talker. In fact, he talked enough for the both of us. He was a lot of fun and didn't seem to mind that I didn't say much. We hung out on the weekends, sometimes going to the store for a soda, or to a movie.

"Hey, Ronnie, you wanna go on a date Saturday?"

I looked at him strangely. Lonnie and I had been going to the movies almost every Saturday for months, but over the past few weeks he had been going out with a girl name Barbara. When he'd asked me to wait for him after school, I'd hoped it was because he wanted to hang out, not to drag me out with him and his girlfriend.

I shook my head. "No thanks," I said.

"Oh come on. Barbara has a sister that wants to meet you."

Meet me? Is he kidding?

I gave him another strange look. I barely talked to anybody at school. I wondered what in the world made him think I'd be able to spend an evening making conversation with a girl.

That would be simply impossible.

"Nawww, Lonnie, that's okay. I don't really want to."

For half an hour we went back and forth on the subject. Lonnie was trying his best to convince me, while I continued to decline the offer.

Eventually he wore me down, and I finally agreed.

As soon as I said yes, I wanted to change my mind, but Lonnie couldn't hear of it. It was Friday afternoon, and I was left to sweat over this decision all night and well into Saturday.

Lonnie and I arrived at the Huber's home at six o'clock sharp. Lonnie's girlfriend, Barbara, opened the door.

"Hi, guys. Come on in," she said. "Good to see you, Ronnie," she smiled.

"Hi." I looked nervously around the room.

Mr. and Mrs. Huber were sitting in the living room and greeted Lonnie when he came in before me.

"This is my friend, Ronnie," he said, introducing us. Both the adults shook my hand and gave me friendly smiles. I relaxed a little, but not much. I still hadn't met Barbara's sister.

"Please have a seat," said Mrs. Huber. "Would you like something to drink?"

"No, ma'am," I answered. My palms were sweaty, and I wiped them nervously on my pants.

"You must be Ronnie," said a pretty brown-haired girl as she walked into the living room. "I'm Charmaine."

I jumped to my feet. "Hi."

She sat down next to me, and we all talked for a few minutes. The Hubers asked me a lot of questions about school, my brother, and the things I was interested in.

It felt a little strange for me. I'd never met any adults that had ever spent that much time listening to kids. I kept my answers short, not wanting to say too much. My past was one topic better kept to myself. I didn't want to tell about all the terrible things that had happened to Vic and me.

"We'd better go," said Barbara, looking at her watch.

"Have a good time, kids," said Mr. Huber. He patted me on the back as he walked us to the door. "Come and visit us again, Ronnie."

"Yes, sir," I mumbled. I doubted that I would go back. Even though being around that family had been nice, I didn't want to get too comfortable. I was too shy when it came to having so much conversation, and I feared that if I stayed too quiet, I'd appear rude.

The four of us walked to the movie theater in twos. Lonnie and Barbara walked a few feet ahead of Charmaine and me and were chatting non-stop. I wasn't sure what to say, but Charmaine kept up conversation and we managed to talk a little. Nevertheless, I was relieved when we settled into the theater seats and the lights went down. I had at least an hour where I wouldn't be expected to say anything. I was used to doing that.

The night at the movies came and went. Much to my surprise, my initial decision to stay away from the Hubers' house didn't stand. Lonnie informed me that Mrs. Huber had invited me to have dinner with them the following week, and I accepted. During dinner, the warmth and harmony at the table made me feel good. The family was so easygoing and kind to one another that I couldn't help but soak it all in like a sponge.

Charmaine and I got along really well. The two of us had figured out after that first trip to the movies that while we were very friendly with each other, neither of us was interested in being boyfriend and girlfriend. Once we'd established that, subsequent outings to the movies and to the drugstore for sodas were much more comfortable.

Though my life experiences were limited, the Hubers were unlike any parents I'd even imagined. They were patient, understanding, and took a real interest in what all their kids had to say. They even extended that patience and interest to me. Before long, I began to look forward to my visits there. All the kids treated me as if I belonged, a feeling I had never experienced. Their acceptance was the most precious thing I'd ever received.

In the days that preceded my eighteenth birthday, I was in a frenzy trying to figure out what I would do for the rest of my life. The policy at ISSC was that children could no longer stay there once they'd reached the age of eighteen. Vic had been required to leave the year before, and now I was faced with the same dilemma.

To say the least, I was very worried about where I would go and even what would become of me. I had limited work experience and not very much money saved. Even though I spent practically every free moment I had at the Hubers', they weren't my family, and I didn't dare think of imposing on them. I didn't have any other family to speak of. In short, things were looking extremely bleak.

Just when I was beginning to think that I'd end up out on the street, the answer came to me. Our last days of school were upon us, and several military recruiters came and visited our class trying to persuade us to join. When the army recruiter came and explained the benefits of service, I decided it was the best option for me. It solved my issues of residency and finance all in one shot. The added aspect of being able to travel also intrigued me. A few days before graduation I signed on the dotted line, and a week later I was sworn in.

On my last night before basic training, the Hubers threw me a surprise going-away party. Lonnie, whom I considered my best friend, was in on the little secret. He and Barbara were still going out and had managed to drag me out on yet another of their dates.

Only that time, it was a decoy. Halfway to the theater, Barbara pretended to feel sick, and we turned around to go back to her house. When I stepped over the threshold the entire family, as well as some of our friends from school, jumped out and yelled, "Surprise!"

To say it was overwhelming was an understatement. I had never been the center of attention for something good before. To see that so many people had come together to see me off made me feel incredible. At the same time I felt a little sad. I was sure that this was the feeling that I was supposed to have known as a child, and to have been deprived of it for as long as I had hurt tremendously. But I pushed those thoughts aside and enjoyed all they had planned for me.

We sang songs, played games, and ate plenty of good food. It was late when our friends from school left. I was preparing to leave myself, thinking the party was over, when Mrs. Huber came out with a chocolate cake.

Each of the Hubers had a small gift for me, and by then, I had a hard time holding back my tears. David gave me a camera to take pictures at my first duty station. April and Charmaine gave me a heavy sweater, and Barbara gave me a scarf. Mr. and Mrs. Huber gave me a small photo album. Inside were pictures of the entire Huber family, and some of Lonnie and me. In the back was the one picture that we had all taken together. There was a lump in my throat that made it hard for me to swallow. I looked around the room at all of them.

"Thank you so much," I said quietly.

"You're welcome, Ronnie," Mrs. Huber said, hugging me tightly. "You take care of yourself, and make sure you come back to visit."

"Yes, ma'am. I will."

The rest of the family took turns hugging me. Lonnie clasped my hand tightly and patted me on the back.

"Good luck, buddy," he said.

Mr. Huber drove me back to ISSC that night. Before I got out of the car, he shook my hand again.

"If you need anything, you can call us, okay?"

I nodded somberly. For the first time I actually felt as if there was someone I could call if I had trouble. I got out of the car and watched as Mr. Huber's car drove away.

When I could no longer see the glow of the taillights, I walked back to my cottage. My bags were already packed, so I slipped out of my clothes and got into bed. I lay awake and thought over the night's events. I was truly going to miss the Hubers, and at that point I almost didn't want to leave. They were like family, and that was what I'd always wanted, a family.

Chapter Seventeen: Finding God

To those of you going through painful times, I pray that you learn to believe in yourself. It doesn't matter what anyone says about you; simply know and believe that you are a unique and a wonderfully made individual. While no person, especially a child, should have to endure the pain and sadness that you may be feeling, know that inside, you are stronger than anything you may face. With God's help you will only grow stronger.

Learn to let go of the past and take hold of God's hand. You can be anything you want to be as long as you believe in yourself. I believe in you and I salute you, the unwanted child.

I was seventeen when I realized that if I didn't take control of my life, I was going to end up on a path of destruction that would inevitably cause the rest of my life to be as miserable as my childhood had been.

The first step in taking control of my life was probably the hardest. The first step of any endeavor is always the most difficult, but the first step required of me, forgiveness, was particularly difficult. I had begun to know God at this time in my life, and the common theme that resounded in my head as I studied the Bible was forgiveness. I remember being stuck on that word for quite some time. I'd had some horrendous experiences in my short life, none of which I felt I could forgive and all of which I knew I would never forget. Still, the course of my life had been so awful, what did I have to lose?

When I took the time to examine all that had transpired, I realized that I was not responsible for the bad things that had happened to me. I had no control over those things. I also realized that all those experiences had left deep scars on my soul and in my heart. I had been abandoned, hurt, deceived, and abused so much that my self-esteem was shot and my faith in others nearly completely eroded. After all, if I had not been able to trust my own parents and caretakers, why on earth would I believe in a stranger?

And so it was from that place that I began my new journey in life. Muddled in confusion, riddled with doubt, and not very hopeful, I decided to give love a try.

We live, then we die!

Sounds simple, doesn't it?

But it is not so simple. It is what we do with our lives between those times that really matters. It seems like a long time when we are young, but as we get older time seems to speed up.

As we start looking back, we see all the time that we wasted away and all the negative things we did and wish we could go back in time and change our mistakes. But we realize that it is an impossible task. All we can do about those mistakes is learn from them and hope that those we hurt will forgive us.

On the positive side, we can look back and see what we have done to make the world a better place. The trick is to do more to help the world, not just for our own sake but also for everyone. When we leave this place we do not know for sure what happens to our spirit. Some say we go to heaven, some say we go to hell, some say we are reincarnated, and some say we stay in limbo.

No matter what happens, one's ultimate fate surely depends on what we do while we are here. I have forgiven those who have hurt me. Because of this, I have been able to find what real love is through God, my wife, and my son. When I reached the age of seventeen, I realized that if I did not take control of my life and put it in God's hands, I would be heading for a disaster.

I immediately told myself that I had no control of what happened in my past. But what happened to me from this point on would be my responsibility. I would be making the decisions, right or wrong, and I would have to take the blame for what I did wrong and credit for what I did right. The decisions would be my own.

What I didn't realize was that my past had left many scars buried deep within me; plus, I was entering the real world without the knowledge of being loved or even loving someone else. I was always considered a loner. I would turn red every time a girl would talk to me, and I would turn even a deeper red when they would mention that my face was turning red.

I had made some friends in my cottage at the Illinois Soldiers and Sailors Children's Home. But since I had been burned so many times before, I couldn't allow anyone else to get close to me. I knew that whoever he or she was, I would be left alone sooner or later. I felt that I was causing people to leave.

After all, from the time I could remember every place I lived, after a short time, I would be moved to another place. I had no self-esteem or self-confidence. I was a poor student in high school, and I knew that at the age of eighteen, I would be forced to leave the children's home. Since I felt that I was not smart enough to get a job in the real world, the only choice I had was to walk the streets, begging, or join the military.

Chapter Eighteen:
Ron Joins the Army

ON THE FIRST OF JUNE 1963, I WENT DOWN TO THE ARMY recruiting office and signed the papers to join the service. The recruiter informed me that I would have to go to Chicago and take a physical and a mental exam. This made me extremely nervous, seeing as I usually failed exams. I went back to the children's home and informed them of the outcome with the recruiting officer. I wanted to say good-bye to my friends in the cottage, but they wouldn't let me. I was told that I would have to stay at the infirmary until I got on the train to Chicago.

The social worker drove me to the train station in Bloomington, Illinois. While I was waiting for my train to arrive, the social worker stated that I could not go back to the Illinois Soldiers and Sailor's Children's home even if I didn't pass the exams. Fear grew within me.

What would I do if I couldn't go in the army? Where would I go and what was going to happen to me?

All I had with me were the clothes on my back and a dollar in my pocket. The train pulled up to the station, and as I boarded it, all I could remember was the social worker saying, "Good-bye, good luck," and that I could not go back to the home if I failed.

The thought of being alone again was different this time. Before, as we moved from one home to another, I had my big brother Victor. This time I was literally alone. My brother was no longer with me, and I had no one to go to if I had a problem. But I was ready to take on the world alone. I knew that God would be with me, but I didn't know what he had planned for me.

All I could do was keep my faith in God. After all, every person on this planet had failed me. I still felt it was my fault, but I could never understand what I was doing wrong. I remember looking out the train window and seeing the children's home in the distance, and I must have fallen asleep, because it seemed like a short time before I heard the conductor announcing the next stop was Chicago Union Station. I looked out the window and saw the tall buildings, and it seemed like the city was swallowing the train as we went underground and soon pulled into the station.

I gathered my papers and looked over the directions that the recruiter gave me, and it looked as if the recruiting station was just a few blocks away from the station. After walking for about twenty minutes, I was standing in front of a tall building with a sign saying "Army Recruiting Center."

I entered the door and there was a counter with an army soldier standing in front of me. I handed the soldier the document, the recruiter handed them back to me, and the soldier pointed to a set of elevators, saying that I should take one of the elevators to the twentieth floor and I would be directed as to where I should go from here. I stepped into the elevator, and when the door opened, I stood there looking into a large room. There were about fifty men sitting around, some talking and others just sitting alone with a stone look on their faces.

"Drop the documents in the in box and take a seat," a rough voice instructed me.

I sat there just thinking of what I would do if I didn't pass the exams. I pictured myself laying on a park bench and begging for money so I could eat. I was scared, but I thought that this was not the first time. I had been in such a position several times while I was growing up. I knew God would help me through this situation, as he had done in the past. It wasn't long before I heard my name being called out with a group of other names. I was asked to fill out several pages of personal information. I started to write my name, Ron Somerville, but as I looked at my birth certificate, which was given to me when I left the children's home, I couldn't believe my eyes—I either had the wrong birth certificate, or my first name had been typed in wrong.

There in front of me was the name Roland Eugene Somerville. I brought it up to the soldier and asked him what I should put down, since I never knew those names. He said that the social security number matched so I wrote down what was on the birth certificate. I went back to my desk and completed the form.

That was the first time I saw my real name. I was always called Ron or Ronnie. But I wrote Roland Eugene Somerville, even though I didn't like it.

The next question was what were my mother's and father's names?

Since I could not recall anyone mentioning their names, I again asked the soldier what I should put down. I could not ever remember what they looked like, let alone what their names were. The next question was who my guardian was. Since I did not have one at the time, I gave him the name of the director at the children's home.

I thought back to the first time I was asked what my mother's and father's names were. I was entering first grade and the teacher asked me to stand up and tell the class what my parents' names were, and when I replied that I didn't know, the whole class broke out in laughter. I hung my head down and slowly walked back to my desk. I didn't see what was so funny.

After I finally completed all the forms and handed them back to the soldier, I went back to my chair. After a few minutes, we were told to go to the classroom where we would be taking an exam. We all found a desk and sat down. Soldiers walked around to each desk and laid down an exam with two pencils. As they handed them out, another soldier told us not to touch anything until he told us to do so. After he explained the rules we were given twenty minutes to complete the exam.

It took me the entire twenty minutes to complete the exam. I put the exam into the box and went back to the waiting room and prayed I passed. While waiting for the results I could see that I was not the only person nervous about the results. The room was very quiet, not like it was before we went in. Every once in a while a name would be called out and the person would go up to the sergeant and then they would leave. I waited for at least an hour before my name was called with several other names. Then I got the good news. We were told that we had passed the written exam and now were required to take the physical.

It felt like a big load was lifted from my shoulders, because I knew I would have no problem with the physical. I spent so many years on that slave farm I knew I was in good physical shape. We went into another room and were told to remove all of our clothes, down to our underwear and shoes. It was like an assembly line. We would walk past one doctor, who would check eyes, ears, and throat, then our feet.

The next stop was our shots. The shot was not like a small needle; it looked more like a gun—the doctor pressed it to our shoulder and pulled the trigger. Before giving us the shot, he warned us not to move because it could pull the skin off your arm.

It was just a few minutes after he started. The man in front of me jumped when the doctor pulled the trigger, and I could see blood dripping down his arm and onto the floor. The man fainted after seeing his blood coming down his arm.

It was my turn next, and I just stood there like a statue as the doctor pulled the trigger. I was surprised that it didn't hurt at all. We then got dressed and went back to the waiting room to wait several more hours for the results. On the final stop, we entered a room where we raised our right hand and took the same oath the President takes when he enters office.

I was now in the U.S. Army—what a relief. I didn't have to sleep on the sidewalk. We were informed that we would be going to Fort Knox, Kentucky, for our basic training. It was getting late, so we were given a food voucher and told to go down to the cafeteria. After eating we were told to go outside and get on the bus parked in front of the building. Night was falling, but it was beautiful seeing the city lights sparkling against the dark starry sky.

We all entered the bus and started our long trip to Fort Knox. The bus trip was a quiet trip. I think many were sad leaving their home and family for the first time. I had no family to miss or worry about who would miss me. I was just wondering what it would be like at basic training and what my job would be in the army. I slowly fell asleep.

Chapter Nineteen: Army Life

A DRILL SERGEANT YELLED FOR US "LAZY BUMS" TO GET OFF THE BUS, grab our bags, and then make a line. I'm sure it looked like a cartoon as everyone ran over each other and the luggage as the drill sergeant barked for us to hurry up.

The drill sergeant gave us the welcome speech, saying that for the next six weeks he would be our mother and father, but by the way he was screaming I didn't think he wanted us to call him Dad. He was going to turn us into real soldiers.

We were then marched to our housing. The building was a large two-story wooden structure built during the Second World War. It consisted of a small single room on each side as we entered, which then opened into a large bay with about fifty bunk beds—twenty-five on each side. The floor was waxed so well that you could see your face reflected from the floor. Then, at the other end of the large room, were the latrine and a set of stairs going up to the second level, which looked the same as the lower level.

The heating system worked on a huge coal furnace, but since it was June, I don't think we needed the heating system. There was no air conditioning system in any of the buildings. The drill sergeant ordered us to lay our stuff on our bunk beds and fall back into formation in two minutes. After everyone returned, we were marched to another building that looked like a large warehouse built around the same time as our billets.

There was a long counter with other solders standing behind the counter. As we walked along the counter, a soldier asked us what size we wore, and if you didn't know your size, he looked through our tee shirts, underwear, fatigues, duffel bag, and finally our boots. We were told to change into our uniforms and put all the rest of our clothes into our duffel bag.

We were then marched to the barbershop. You need to remember that this was in the sixties, when long hair was in style. My hair was already a flat top, because that was the only kind of hairstyle you could have at the children's home. After our haircuts, everyone looked completely bald, and some were not too happy about that. We then were marched back to our billets. We didn't slow down until about nine o'clock.

The next six weeks were brutal for some and worse for others, if that was possible. I think most of them had problems with being yelled at for at least eighteen hours a day. I found that didn't bother me so much, because my whole life had been like that, and now I was being paid for it.

I completed basic training, and we had to march on the parade field in front of the commander. Most of the men had their family come down for their graduation. When we marched past the grandstand, we were given the command "eyes right." I looked at all the people sitting there. There was not a single person I knew.

After the parade, all the soldiers linked up with their family and again I had no one to care about what I had completed. There was just complete emptiness. You would think I would have been used to it by that point.

After graduation from basic training, we received our AIT (Advanced Individual Training) orders for the specialized school we were to be trained in. My specialized school was field communications or radio technician. My school was in Fort Jackson, South Carolina. I picked up my orders and bus ticket and soon was headed for South Carolina. Until basic training I'd never been out of the state of Illinois, and now I was going even further. I was looking forward to the trip.

I arrived at Fort Jackson, and when I got off the bus I looked for my duffel bag, which should not have been too hard to find because we stenciled our name in big letters on the outside. The bag was nowhere in sight, so the bus driver said that it was probably put on the wrong bus, but that it should arrive soon. So I had to check into my unit without any clothes except for what I was wearing. I never did receive my duffel bag, and they had to re-issue me all new clothes.

The school was very good, and my only problem was learning Morse code. For four hours every day we listened to dots and dashes. Some of us were talking Morse code in our sleep.

After completing radio school, I was sent to Field Wireman School. I acquired a lot of respect for those pole climbers who climb up and down those telephone poles daily. We were given a set of gaffs—it was like tying a spike to the inside of your foot—then we'd stick one gaff into the side of the pole, lock our knee, and stick the other on the other side of the pole. The one big problem with this was that I couldn't get my knee to lock, because I was shaking so much. After falling about twenty times, I was finally able to get to the top of the ninety-foot pole.

After completing the school, I waited for orders to ship out to Europe.

I was painting the boiler room when I heard over the radio that President Kennedy had been shot. Shocked, I dropped my paintbrush and rushed into the day room, where the television was. I watched TV as the story played out. They continuously showed the footage in which the President's head slumped forward, Jackie reached out to her husband, and the secret service agent jumped on the back of the car as it sped up to the emergency room. We all waited quietly, and some of us had tears running down our cheeks as we heard the announcer report that the President of the United States had been shot and killed. It seemed like the whole world had stopped. There wasn't a sound on the base.

We followed the story as it played out, from Oswald getting shot on TV up to the funeral of our President in Washington D.C. It seemed like weeks went by before normal work started up. I received my assignment to go to Europe and was looking forward to it. We all went out to the beer garden to celebrate.

I never drank alcohol, so my comrades thought it would be fun watching me get drunk. It didn't take very long. I think I passed out after my third pitcher. I remember waking up in my bunk bed and having to go to the latrine. I started going down the steps and woke up at the bottom of the stairs.

One of my friends said that he thought I broke my arm and should go to the dispensary to have it checked out. Still drunk, I walked into the dispensary, and the corps man stated that he could smell alcohol on my breath. He went to get some mouthwash and told me to rinse my mouth out before the doctor saw me. I could be in serious trouble if the doctor found out, he said.

Instead of washing my mouth out, I drank the whole bottle. Within a few minutes I ran for the bathroom to throw up. The next morning I woke up with a cast on my arm and a major headache.

Chapter Twenty:
New Beginnings

ONE MORNING, I WAS GIVEN A TICKET TO FLY TO NEW YORK. I HAD never flown before and eagerly anticipated the flight. I boarded the plane and found a seat next to the window. At last, the plane taxied down the runway. As we went faster, my whole body was pushed back into the seat. The plane lifted from the runway and the ground disappeared. It was great. Only a few months before, I had never been in anything but a car, and now I had been on a train, a plane, and soon a ship. I had made the right choice by joining the army.

We landed in New York and boarded a bus to the shipyard. After collecting our bags, we started up the gangplank. The name painted on the side of the ship was USNS *Geiger*. We stored our gear down in the lower deck, where the sleeping area, consisting of about fifty hammocks, was located. I didn't realize that the trip would take two weeks. Everyone was given some chores to do but me, because I had a cast on my arm. By the time we pulled away from the dock it was nightfall. I watched as the lights of New York slowly faded away into the darkness. Since it was so noisy, it wasn't relaxing for some. We didn't get many chances to get above deck, but when we did, it was quite beautiful.

After about a week, we docked in Barcelona, Spain. I was looking forward to getting off the ship to see the area, but no such luck. Since I didn't do any chores while we were crossing the Atlantic, I was assigned to watch everyone's gear.

We only spent about two days in Barcelona before we shipped off to Germany. We arrived in Bremen, Germany, disembarked, and walked with all our gear to a waiting train. The ride was wonderful. I had never ridden a train like this, and its steady drone lulled me to a restful sleep that first night. When I woke up the next morning and looked out the train window, I witnessed the most beautiful scene in my life: the sun was out and there were the largest mountains I ever imagined, with snow-covered peaks.

My final destination was Wildflicken, Germany.

Wildflicken was a basic training camp for the German soldiers and for other American troops stationed in Germany. The billets, built during the Second World War, had rooms heated with a potbelly stove. I learned how to stock the stove so it would last all night, keeping the bucket of coal full.

The base sat on the side of a mountain. After a large snowfall, it was impossible to get on or off base. I worked as the communication chief and chief of the base MARS radio station.

I loved the food and beer in Germany. I suspect it was my love for German beer that caused me to stop drinking when I got back from Germany—I couldn't stand the taste of American beer.

I was stationed for six years at Wildflicken. I met my first wife, Anne, while I was there. She was the first girl I ever had sex with. Not that I hadn't tried before her; she was just the first to let me. Her parents kicked me out of their home, but not before I had gotten her pregnant. I didn't want my child to be brought up like I was, without knowing her parents, so I married Anne, even though many people told me that she only wanted to marry me so she could get to the United States. This seemed to be a common practice for many girls who wanted to get to America. My sister Barb, who was stationed with her husband, Lonnie, in Germany, informed me that Anne had told her the same thing; she was marrying me to get to the United States.

Barb passed on the information that her family wanted me to be their legal son, and she asked me if I wanted to be her brother. A large lump filled me up. I had dreamed for seventeen years that *someone* would adopt me. I told Barb that this would be the greatest honor anyone could bestow upon me.

When I was reassigned to Colorado Springs, I was given thirty days leave. Anne and I boarded an airplane to Normal, Illinois. The Huber family welcomed us with open arms. The next day, we went to the courthouse in Bloomington, Illinois, where I stood in front of the judge. He asked me if I wanted to be the son of the Huber family, and without hesitation I replied, "Yes."

As I looked out into the courtroom, I noted a cold stare emitting from Anne's eyes. She had previously told me that she didn't want me to be adopted by the Hubers, but I told her that she didn't have a choice in this. I never did find out why she didn't want the Huber family to adopt me. It didn't matter. I finally had a family that wanted me with no strings attached.

But there were other problems I had to work out. I already suspected that Anne was marrying me to get to the United States. But I still felt I had to do the right thing.

Even God had tried to warn me. The night before the wedding, there was a huge snowstorm that knocked out the power all over the base. When we arrived at the church, there was no electricity. No one from my unit came to the wedding.

I stayed with her for eleven years, and the only good that came out of that marriage were my two daughters. I knew the day I married her that it was a mistake, but I was responsible for the child she was carrying, and nothing could change that fact.

My oldest daughter was born in Colorado Springs, where I was stationed to prepare for Vietnam combat. Six months after my daughter Susan was born, I received my orders. Anne returned to Germany with my daughter and lived with her parents while I went to Vietnam in 1967. I flew out of San Francisco in November of that same year.

Chapter Twenty-One:
Vietnam

As I PEERED OUT INTO THE DARKNESS FROM MY OFFICE WINDOW suddenly I froze. I stiffened. My heart began to pulsate. Fear spread through my body like wild fires rolling across deep hillside forests. My hands shook as I heard the crackle of gunfire ring out—the faraway and long ago barrages, *fft fft fft*, spitting through the clumps of thick Asian greens.

Charlie was seemingly everywhere—on every tree, under every bush, in every clearing, under the searing sun, in every bombed-out shelter. Still standing, waiting for their chance to kill me. I felt their eyes on me, their hands at my throat. They were always within striking distance; their weapons were pointed at my back. I felt their breath down my neck.

A couple of shots whizzed by my right ear. *Fft fft fft fft.* I never actually saw Charlie, but they were lurking in the shadows of a war I didn't want to die in.

It was Vietnam. 1968. Tet: the battle that changed the war and history.

North Vietnamese leaders had no choice. They were under heavy pressure to mount an all-out major military operation against the forces of the American-backed, pro-western South Vietnam to win the war or risk being unable to withstand heavy losses inflicted indefinitely. With Ho Chi Minh near death and LBJ's war growing increasingly unpopular at home, nevertheless, the north needed a decisive victory before its leader died.

And so on January 31, the first day of the lunar New Year, Vietnam's most popular holiday, the Tet Offensive shocked the world, as the Vietcong rebel forces in concert with regular North Vietnamese soldiers launched a series of surprise attacks.

In a well-coordinated operation, they attacked the presidential palace in the capital, Saigon, the airport, the ARVN headquarters, and even battled their way onto the grounds of the American embassy, catching the United States off guard. They struck in scores of cities, towns, and hamlets. When the operation ended, it was the turning point in the war that we were going to lose.

At age eighteen , I realized I had fought and won one war—for my heart and soul. Now I faced a second war—this one for my country and for my very life. If I made it out, I would have one last war facing me—a war for a life.

My unit was guarding a major ammunition dump deployed just outside Long Bing camp on assignment to escort a Marine unit to Da Nang. The military planners had just replaced the U.S. guards, rigging the dump with a unit that had just arrived in country. The guards were informed that if they came under attack, they were to evacuate the towers and get into the bunkers.

When Charlie attacked, the American unit was so scared that they forgot to take their weapons with them. Charlie walked right from the back door and killed every guard in sight at the dump. Our convoy was already loaded and moving out the front gate while Charlie was closing in from the back.

Our first assignment was to convoy from Long Ben to Saigon, which was about twenty miles away. The Tet Offensive was just starting, and Charlie was already destroying Long Ben. As we moved out, we watched as one of the mortar rounds blew up the chaplain's hooch. I heard later that no one survived.

We moved as fast as we could down the highway to Saigon, rounds going off all around us. The only firepower we had was our M16 rifles, and here we were with truckloads of ammo. We had radio communications, but with all that was going on in Long Ben and Saigon, we couldn't expect much support.

We were getting close to the bridge that crossed over the Saigon River and the navy port with the LST, a flat-bottom navy ship. We were to board about two hundred meters from the bridge. When our last vehicle crossed the bridge, one of our tanks was ready to get on the bridge to protect our behind. We were thankful they were there.

As soon as we crossed, a large unit of Vietcong came across the bridge, loaded with satchel charges. We watched the tank open up on them, and it seemed as though nothing could stop them. Arms and legs flew everywhere, but they continued to attack. The tank was able to save the bridge, and we were loaded onto the LST. We watched mortar fire across the Saigon River, more than three hundred meters away. They were firing into an ARVN, South Vietnam, shoulder camp, which meant that the rounds were going over our ship. Our ship was loaded with trucks full of ammunition. One round would have blown up our whole ship.

I was assigned as the security sergeant while we were aboard. While I was checking out the security, I saw our commanding officer getting ready to fire from our ship to where he thought the mortars were being fired from. I caught him before he pulled the trigger and grabbed his rifle, informing him that if he had fired across into the village, they would start firing upon our ship and that just one round would have sunk our ship.

Finally, the navy had cleared the river, and we moved out to the China Sea. As we entered the sea, there were private ships waiting to go into Saigon. It took us a couple of days before we reached the port of Ad Nang.

The Tet Offensive was still going strong, and we heard gunfire all around us. We unloaded the LST and started our convoy up Highway One toward Happy Valley, which was about ten miles north of Ad Nang. As we passed the Ad Nang air base, we could smell a strong odor of embalming fluid and saw pallets of silver coffins getting ready to be loaded for the States.

On a plane back to the base, I remember thinking that I wished I could have replaced just one of those soldiers. After all, I had never had anyone who loved me or cared what happened to me. Most of those soldiers had a loving family waiting for them. They deserved to be able to go back to those who loved and wanted them.

What had I done with my life?

It had been a long, mournful hunt for an elusive love, the love of a mother and father who could not put down the bottle long enough to lift up their child—to discover me, to caress me, to truly love me and assure me that all my demons would go away.

We finally reached our base camp. We were the only army unit at the camp, and the rest were all Marines. I was sent out on many missions into Happy Valley, where our main job was to support the Marines. I never went on R and R, because we could not afford to leave. Our camp received fire almost every day. The only fireworks on the Fourth of July were the trip flares that showed us where the Vietcong were trying to slip into our camp.

I spent exactly one year there, until I finally received orders to return to the States.

Nothing had prepared me for the greeting of protesters waiting for us when we landed. That hit me like a load of bricks. We were told to get out of our uniforms, because everyone hated soldiers. The pain was so great. I remembered how the soldiers were celebrated from the Second World War as heroes, but we had to hang our heads in shame, being called "baby-killers" and having stones thrown at us.

I am so happy to see the soldiers coming back from Afghanistan and Iraq as the heroes they are. The excuse I get is that they weren't drafted while the soldiers from Vietnam were. I wasn't drafted. It made no difference if they were drafted or not; they still went to support our country. They did not deserve to be called baby-killers.

Even after over forty years, it still leaves a scar in my heart. The interesting thing is that many of those protesters are now sending their children off to war. At least they are bringing their children home as heroes.

Chapter Twenty-Two:
Family Lost and Found

I WAS GIVEN A THIRTY-DAY PASS AND WENT TO MY NEW FAMILY home in Normal, Illinois. The Huber family had a yellow ribbon wrapped around the big tree in our front yard with a huge sign saying, "Welcome Home, Son, from Vietnam." I was proud to be a soldier again. My first wife didn't return from her parents' home in Germany until a couple of weeks later. I never understood why, since there were several flights leaving Germany every day. When I finally looked into my daughter's eyes, I saw that she didn't know who I was.

Nor was the greeting I received from my wife a loving one. It was like two strangers meeting.

I received orders for Fort Bragg, North Carolina, and within a year my second daughter, Kristina, was born. My first wife and I were together for eleven years marked by estrangement and indifference. I stayed in the marriage because of my daughters, even though I realized the relationship was harming them. I will admit a lot of it was my fault. I didn't know what love was, nor did I know how to give love. You can't give what you never received.

To help make more money, I applied for a job as a disc jockey at a local radio station. I was surprised that I got the job, because I had never been a DJ. The first time I was on the air was comical. I missed cue commercials, records, and messed up on the news. It was a Sunday and I was completely by myself. I was nervous enough, when all of a sudden the chief engineer walked in on me and started yelling, asking me who I was. He told me that he had not approved my going on the air and told me to leave the station.

I didn't know what to do, so I turned down the control console, walked out of the station, and went home. When I got home my phone was ringing, and when I answered it, the voice on the other end was pleasant. It was the station manager. He asked me what had happened, and I explained that the chief engineer had tossed me out of the station. He apologized for the misunderstanding and asked me if I would come back, assuring me that he had worked everything out with the chief engineer.

I returned and finished my first day as a DJ. I guess I was okay, because I continued working as a part time DJ for eight more years. Being a DJ helped me break away from my shyness and gave me a lot of confidence. I enjoyed taking calls from my listeners and got a chance to meet many great country stars, like Loretta Lynn, Conway Twitty, Dolly Parton, and many more.

The situation at home continued to get worse, with my marriage disintegrating, but since I played soldier during the day and a DJ at night and weekends, I didn't spend much time there. I really missed my daughters, but I felt this was better for them. I finally left the house with just my clothes. I wanted to make sure that my daughters had everything they needed, and I paid child support until they were both eighteen years old.

Anne married an officer just a few months after the divorce was finalized. She told my daughter's school that I might try to kidnap them and asked them to notify her if I came anywhere near the school. It was a very hostile divorce. The reason she had told the children I would try to kidnap them was that she didn't want me to communicate with my daughters in any way.

Being just an E-5 in the army, I was not making much money and had to go back to court many times, because I wasn't able to pay the bills and the child support. All I could do was send what I had. I finally had to file for bankruptcy, and then I was able to pay what the court had ordered. I was relieved when it was finally over.

They all soon shipped off to Germany. My oldest daughter made sure that I knew where they went. There was no way I could have gone over to visit them because of my financial situation, so I had no way to visit them for years. I could tell that I had lost my daughters forever. It was the only thing that my first wife could have taken from me, and it was the thing that hurt me the most.

From the little bit of communication we did have, I leaned that she had succeeded in her mission. I would have never seen them again had it not been for my daughter Susan's first husband abandoning her. Susan had nowhere to go. Her mother was in Germany, so she could not go there, and I had told them if they ever needed me, they could contact the Huber family in Illinois. They would always know where I was.

I was pleasantly surprised to hear from her and assured her that she was always welcome. I didn't know she had a child until she called. I was now a grandpa and was happy to get to see my grandson, Christopher, for the first time.

In 1983, I was retired from the military and lived in Maryland working for the federal government.

I met my second wife through a dating service I joined after I retired from the army. She said she fell in love with my voice. I was glad, because there wasn't much else to offer. My honey knew about my daughters. I told her many times that I missed them. When I told her that Susan needed a place to stay, she was more than happy to help to take her in. I helped Susan land a job with our agency and get back on her feet. She seemed to be happy, and so did Christopher. I was happy to have them back in my life. Even though she seemed happy, she still seemed to be a little distant. I figured this was mainly due to her divorce. She had no self-confidence, and I tried to help her get some self-esteem, hoping that a job would help.

But as soon as her mother came back from Germany, Susan grew cold and distant with me. She moved back with her mother as fast as she could. The last words I remember her saying were that she hated me. I am sure she felt she had a good reason, and I tried to apologize for anything I had done wrong.

Susan knows where I live, and my home is always open for her, but it has been more than ten years since I have heard from her or my grandson. Kristina was never close to me. I pray that God is watching over them and they find happiness and true love.

Chapter Twenty-Three:
Resolving the Past

WHEN I WAS IN MY FORTIES, I WANTED TO KNOW ONCE AND FOR ALL why my real parents had left, why I was put in the system.

Computers had become much more advanced, and searching for my family became easier. I searched for all the Somervilles in the United States. I had my birth certificate, which had my parents' names and names of other brothers, and I figured that the Illinois Soldiers' and Sailors' Children's Home would have all the documents I needed to track them down. Unfortunately, the home was closed down in the seventies.

The next move was the State Capitol Hall of Records. It helped living in Washington, D.C. I contacted a friend, who located the records from the children's home. They were buried deep down in the basement. He was able to locate not only all my records but also my brother, Victor's.

Since I was in the system from the time I was three years old until I was seventeen, the files were really thick. It was fascinating reading all the information from the first social worker who took on the case, seeing the court order making me a ward of the state, seeing what all the foster parents had to say to the social workers (which was far from what was really going on), and hearing the opinions of the cottage parents in the children's homes and my parents.

The court order stated that Vic and I could not be adopted.

When I talked with my mother forty years later, she said that she made sure I could not be adopted. My reply was that they never came back to see us or even write to us. I told her about the abuse we received while we were in the foster care system. My mother did not say much to me.

Before she died, she told my Aunt Mary that she hoped I never found my brothers. My Aunt Mary died a few years later, and I still have not found my brothers. I did not have anger toward her, even though the documents stated that they could take Vic and me but not Ralph Jr. I am sure my brothers were adopted, because some of the documents state that they were adopted out.

I returned to Frankfort to show my son and wife the farm where I was raised, and the owner mentioned that Mrs. Borg was living in the town of Frankfort. I had him contact her. The visit was very short, because her ill health prevented her from speaking. Mrs. Borg had come down with a bad case of osteoporosis and was bedridden. I talked to her before she died, and she was still a bitter woman.

The lady who was taking care of her near the end of her life told me that Mrs. Borg had left Vic and me some money in her will.

It wasn't long after that that I received word from the lady that Mrs. Borg had passed away. There wasn't going to be a funeral, but her nephews were going to lay her remains next to her brother. I told them I wanted to use the money she gave me to fly to Illinois to attend the ceremony. I called Vic and informed him of her death, but he wanted nothing to do with her, even though he lived just a few miles away from where she was to be put to rest.

On the day they lowered Mrs. Borg's body into the earth, I stood there and listened as her minister gave a short eulogy. His words faded away as I looked around. Only six other people attended. Not one tear was shed; there were merely glazed looks on everyone's faces.

My attention was drawn toward the golden urn holding the ashes of this cruel woman who had tormented a vulnerable child for eight long years. Her nephews lowered the urn in the ground. It was like looking down the dark funnel of a tornado.

Memories came flooding back in a bundle of mixed emotions. From the first day when the social worker pulled the car up the gravel driveway, walking up to an old gray farmhouse where Mrs. Borg reluctantly agreed to take my brother and me in, those days of being worked to death and yelled at, until a tractor accident would ultimately give us our release from eight years of living hell.

It was a long time before Vic and I would get back together. While I was in basic training, Vic had contacted the Hubers asking how he could get in touch with me. They gave him my address and we started back where we left off. I was so happy to have my big brother back. He informed me that he tried to go in the army also, and we found that at one point we were stationed within a few buildings of each other. I was in one unit and he was in the unit across the street from me. Shortly after that, he was transferred out because of a medical problem.

My brother Vic likes reading my books, but he wants to be left alone. He has been married for over forty years, has two children, and several grandchildren. He ended up with a great family, and we talk to each other at least once a month.

I am still looking for the brothers I never knew.

Chapter Twenty-Four:
The Recovery

EVERY ONE OF US MAKES HIS OWN PERSONAL HISTORY. THIS IS OUR birthright. The core part of our personal history is made long before we are born. We all come into this world too late to start our history and merely join our history in progress. Our mothers and fathers as well as our ancestors begin our history, and we craft the final chapters. We are born into a thousand genetic preconditions, predispositions, and natures we did not choose and cannot control. These were chosen for us by people we never met. Every day, more pages are added. Hardly ever is it written down on paper. Rather, it is reported, recorded, and stored along the endless continuum of our vast memory.

For some, there is chapter called "The Recovery."

And so it was for Ron Huber.

Ron broke out of his reverie from his spacious government office overlooking the storied Washington Mall when the telephone rang. He looked at his watch. This is going to be an important day at work.

Seven forty-five AM.

He picked up the receiver and listened to the deep baritone voice at the other end before he answered.

"Good morning to you too, Mr. Secretary."

He paused.

"Yes, my report is ready to go. Nine o'clock? I'll be there."

Ron hung up the phone.

The clock moved so slowly, but at last it was time to go.

As he was leaving, his gaze settled on the enclosed glass case hanging on his wall that displayed his numerous combat medals.

Why not? he muttered to himself. _Why not read the inscriptions on the plaques hanging next to the glass case one more time before the big meeting?_

One was inscribed, "Who's Who—Madison Honors Ronald Huber, member of the year to appear in the 2008–2009 edition of the _Madison Who's Who Registry of Executives and Professionals_, having demonstrated exemplary achievement and distinguished contributions to the business community." The other inscription awarded by Strathmore's Who's Who read, "The recipient named above has been selected as a lifetime member in Strathmore's Who's Who. Acceptence is granted based on the member's leadership achievement and dedication in their profession or industry."

"Not bad for a throwaway child," he said quietly in the stillness of his empty office.

Just minutes before his big presentation to the board, his mind wandered back to visions of the wicked "Mama Borg" displaying her artistry of horror, frantically whipping up on a frightened innocent child on a rundown farm somewhere in the vast furnace of hell. He summoned up imaginary scenes of the extensive, unmandated transgressions of an uncaring foster care system whose savage, ruinous rule of dominion and oppression doomed thousands of lost kids forever.

A powerful force inside him burst forth, and with a renewed sense of purpose, Ron walked out of the office and turned right.

At first he strolled down the empty hallway. Then, with a strut of a champion, he playfully and proudly swaggered toward the imposing double glass doors to deliver the most important report of his rising career.

Ron stopped near the elevator and felt the close presence of his maker, who had always stood by his side in his rage and pain as unspeakable acts were committed against him, as his fragile heart broke so many times, so many years ago.

Is that to be my legacy? Is that my heritage?

Ron then smiled slightly and shook his head faintly as he resumed his walk.

God, don't ever leave me. I'll never leave you.

He remembered his motto nestled in his mind.

"If you believe it, it will happen. If you don't believe, it will not happen."

The exact moment he entered the bustling secretary's outer office, he reflected again on his "rats to riches" saga. Thought of that kid who was constantly whipped, scorned, slapped repeatedly in the back of his head, the boy who had to feed the chickens, milk the cows, lug that yellow hay from morning to night and repeat the chore the next day and the next until he, like Sisyphus, could not stand any longer.

With the cacophony of his disastrous youth still ringing in his ears and his secrets sequestered forever from public view, Ron stepped into the secretary's inner office, smiling broadly.

"Good morning, again, Ron. Sit. Please. Coffee?"

Ron took a seat and nodded in appreciation. The Secretary leaned back in his chair.

"Ron, how long did it take you to do the report?"

Ron pursed his lips and looked straight into the kind eyes of the white haired secretary. With a wrinkled brow he spoke, almost whispering his confession.

"Sixty-two years, sir. Sixty-two years."

Epilogue

So where's the light? I cannot see.
I feel its glow shine over me.
What will be my destiny?
Worshiping the adventure of my life relentlessly.
Yet will I be loved?
I found my Eden, a gift from above.

The irony of my life is that while I had no mother in my youth, I have a mother as I approach my senior citizen years.

In fact, I have a hundred mothers.

Feeling the nearness, the power and greatness of God when the people who I thought loved me trespassed against me is my mother.

Walking hand in hand with my loved one through a windswept leafy glade, following an autumn rain, is my mother.

So where's the light? I cannot see.
I feel its glow shine over me.

What will be my destiny?
Worshiping the adventure of my life relentlessly.
Yet will I be loved?
I found my Eden, a gift from above.

Shrugging off the entrenched madness from the massive traumatic moments of my young life is my mother.

Surviving the trilogy of hateful, vengeful, evil people is my mother.

The joy of viewing scattered rows of daggers of icicles dancing on snow-covered tree branches in an endless forest at holiday time is my mother.

Slowly sipping a glass of a fine, full-bodied red wine with my candlelit dinner out on my red brick patio on a cool summer evening with my close friends is my mother.

So where's the light? I cannot see.
I feel its glow shine over me.
What will be my destiny?
Worshiping the adventure of my life relentlessly.
Yet will I be loved? I found my Eden, a gift from above.

Watching my son reach manhood is my mother.

Living a life next to my God is my mother, and yes, witnessing a man in shorts sink a three from half court at the buzzer to win a championship is my mother.

For the richness, goodness, and successful life I have lived; for the illusive love I ultimately found is my mother.

So where's the light. I cannot see.
I feel its glow shine over me.
What will be my destiny?
Worshiping the adventure of my life relentlessly.
Yet will I be loved?
I found my Eden, a gift from above.

About the Author

MR. BLOTNER HAS ENJOYED A LONG AND DISTINGUISHED AWARD-winning career in journalism, which has spanned six decades as a city hall newspaper reporter, news writer, editor, radio production specialist, and on-air announcer in the Boston and Washington D.C. areas.

He and his wife, Diana, reside in the Maryland suburbs.

From the Author:

I DECIDED TO TAKE UP THE CAUSE FOR THE THOUSANDS OF FACELESS victims of the brutal foster care system after my colleague and friend, Ron Huber, told me about some of the shocking atrocities he and his brother had to endure in these types of homes in the forties and fifties. Although we rode the same subway train to work for years—before dawn—got off at the same subway station, walked the same eight minutes to the same federal office building, and took elevators to the same floor at the same time, we did not know each other very well. Then, inevitably, one morning we simply struck up a conversation.

Over time we would talk of many things on those dark morning walks to work, including his career in the military. On one such morning, he casually informed me that he receives regular treatments at Walter Reed Army Hospital for the osteoporosis he still suffers from the ravages of malnutrition as an abandoned and unwanted foster care child. I talked about my career as a cub journalist. I comically informed him that my first news writing job at a radio station in my home town of Haverhill, Massachusetts, consisted of calling up the local funeral homes, writing up the obits, and putting them on the air.

To this Ron replied, "That sounds like a dead-end job to me."

Ron then confided in me that he had spent part of his childhood in two inhuman foster homes, describing the mental and physical abuse and torture he and Vic staggered through.

I bluntly but diplomatically inquired why he had not killed someone to take out his hatred and anger, why had he not manifested some trace of asocial behavior?

His reply was that serving in Vietnam had turned his life around. His life story shocked and saddened me, and it raised my concerns for the thousands of other victims out there. I wanted to help in some small way, hence my book.

So I lift my glass in tribute to the once-wretched and oppressed who harbor hopes and expectations, that my small contribution might someday empower them to break the chains of the past, rise up like Ron, and flourish in their adult environment.

Ron and I still take the subway to work each morning, standing on that same darkened subway platform through Washington's blinding rains of autumn, penetrating cold of winter, cool breezes of glorious spring, and the Death Valley heat of summer, although we are both contemplating retirement.

In evaluating the incongruous plots and subplots of his life, Ron continues to juxtapose the searing pain he endured in the brutal foster care system with his countless achievements. His journey back to that vast wilderness of his wasted youth on that frigid winter morning will be repeated again and again. His suffering is without end. Like frigid snow-capped mountains and the lush steamy jungles below, it is eternal. He fought three wars and won them all. But he must battle his past every day.

He will always take imaginary photos in his mind of a family he craved for but never had, and to this day when he sees a child walking with its parents—with a smile, holding hands—he wishes that he had been that child.

For me, writing this meaningful book was the chance of a lifetime. But far more significantly, I had the good fortune of making a good friend and being a good friend.

And there you have it.

To my friend:

Vos usquequaque sentio subluceo diligo.
(May you always feel the glow of love.)

www.ingramcontent.com/pod-product-compliance
Lightning Source LLC
Chambersburg PA
CBHW022249290526
45785CB00015B/432